Dog Training

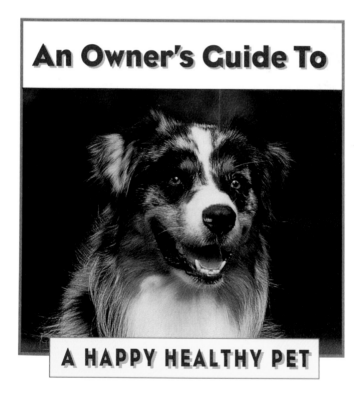

An Owner's Guide To

A HAPPY HEALTHY PET

Howell Book House

Howell Book House
A Simon & Schuster Macmillan Company
1633 Broadway
New York, NY 10019

Macmillan Publishing books may be purchased for business or sales promotional use.
For information please write: Special Markets Department, Macmillan Publishing
USA, 1633 Broadway, New York, NY 10019.

Library of Congress Cataloging-in-Publication Data
Ammen, Amy.
Dog training / by Amy Ammen.
    p. cm.—(An owner's guide to a happy healthy pet)
Includes bibliographical references

ISBN 0-87605-564-1
1. Dogs—Training.   I. Title   II. Series
SF431.A428   1998
636.7'0835—dc21   98-12611
                        CIP

Manufactured in the United States of America
10 9 8 7 6 5 4 3 2 1

Series Director: Amanda Pisani
Series Assistant Director: Jennifer Liberts
Book Design: Michele Laseau
Cover Design: Iris Jeromnimon
Photography:
    Front cover photo, inset photo and title page photo by Winter Churchill
        Photography; back cover photo courtesy of Amy Ammen.
    Joan Balzarini: 7, 98
    Cheryl Primeau: 15, 101, 106, 111, 123
    Bob Schwartz: 2–3, 5, 10, 14, 24–25, 26, 35, 37, 78, 82, 84, 89, 93, 94, 95, 99, 104,
        107, 113, 119, 120
    Faith Uridel: 18
    All other photos courtesy of Amy Ammen.
Production Team: Chris Van Camp, Clint Lahnen, Angel Perez, Dennis Sheehan,
    Terri Sheehan

Dogs in training:

*Charlotte Allman's Petite Basset Griffon Vendeen, Phoebe; Amy Korta's Old English Sheepdog,
Lucy; Karla J. Ebert's Rottweiler, Carly; Marilyn Patrick's Australian Shepherd, Comet; Jan
Plagenz's Doberman Pinscher, Alex; Wendy Sostock's Canaan Dog, Esprit; Bobbie Oxley's
Norwegian Elkhounds, Ranger and Jamie; Joan Mullen's Belgian Malinois, Nala; Edward
and Nancy Bower's Flat-Coated Retrievers, Tina, Rosie and Keeper; Amy Ammen's Tibetan
Spaniel, BJ; Sue Hanson's Bullmastiff, Tank; Irish Setter, Matthew; and Border Terrier, Bear.*

Contents

Before You

part one

Start

External Features of a Dog

Skull
Stop
Muzzle
Cheek
Shoulder
Forearm
Wrist
Crest
Neck
Withers
Elbow
Dewclaw
Pastern
Back
Loin
Stifle or knee
Toes
Croup
Hock

chapter 1

The **Right** **Approach**

Before you begin training your dog, re-member that the following key points will unlock the door to success. Refer to them whenever you feel stuck or out of touch with your dog.

1. Make sure that your dog is healthy, fit and well groomed.

2. Say what you mean and mean what you say.

3. Take the time to learn how to train, and then practice with your dog diligently.

4. Concentrate while practicing the assigned lessons, and your dog will concentrate on you.

5. Focus on your goals, not your rate of progress.

6. Use one command for one action so that your dog won't be confused.

7. Recognize that dogs have far more potential than limitations—and that *your* dog's potential is limited only by your dedication.

8. Remember that dogs live for the moment; instead of correcting bad behavior after the fact, recreate the situation and correct at the proper time, in the proper way.

Love Is Not Enough

Maybe you've been led to believe that if you love your dog and he loves you, he won't be unruly. But take it from Tina Turner: "What's Love Got To Do With It?" The truth is, love has nothing to do with your dog's ability to obey, but understanding does. Your dog has to understand what you expect through the way you communicate. Your message may seem obvious to you. But unless you convey it in terms he understands, he will misinterpret and fail to please you—no matter how devoted he may be.

Sadly, every day loving people abandon loving dogs at shelters and on farms because of behavior problems— problems that are both correctable and preventable. They don't understand that love doesn't educate dogs; research, practice and perseverance do. Love is a great beginning but, by itself, it's shallow and self-centered. Dedicate yourself to training, even when the going gets tough, and your dog will return your kindness endlessly. Just do it!

Your Dog Is Trainable

It's tempting to sit back and evaluate how responsive your dog will be to training, but don't! It's too easy to imagine seeing the word "untrainable" stamped on his ID tag, especially if your dog is always in his own little world, not really looking at you, seeking praise or acknowledging your existence. The fact is, very few dogs are beyond hope, incapable of learning the basics and delighting you. And no, you don't have to forgo every other interest in your life to accomplish training your dog.

No doubt about it: Lyn's 8-week-old Lab puppy was adorable. But her behavior wasn't: Although most Lab pups are relaxed and sociable at that age, Tilly was a real wasp. Often when strange dogs were near, she stiffened, raised her hackles and growled with an intensity and frequency I'd rarely seen in any breed at that age. And she was no better at home; the mere sight of Lyn's refined felines was enough to send Tilly into a frenzy.

Lyn's fears were warranted: Left to her own devices, Tilly would probably grow to a cranky maturity—and probably die from something other than a natural death.

Fortunately, Lyn was smart enough to take her puppy to training, ultimately molding her into not just a good dog, but an absolutely delightful dog.

Lyn was also gifted with a perfect attitude toward the task: "I really enjoyed working with Tilly, and watching her learn," she told me after finishing puppy and basic training. "It's just as though I had kids. I'd want them to go to movement class, learn art techniques and play music—appreciate and comprehend the simple joys of life and of learning."

Give your dog a chance— he is trainable!

Just give him a chance. The truth is, every dog deserves the opportunity to learn—even if we believe that he lacks great potential, effort is more important than talent.

Cinder was a young adult Labrador/terrier mix, a stray adopted by the Rands from the Humane Society. She was sweet-tempered but super-charged, with her primary ambition centered around sprinting as fast and as far as her long legs would take her. And when she wasn't taking off on her owners, she attended to such tasks at soiling, stealing, chewing, jumping and barking at anything that moved.

A week after adopting Cinder, the Rands called me for help—primarily for off-lead control and boundary training. The Rands had no experience in bringing an out-of-control dog under control; nor were they exceptionally talented trainers. But their drive and conviction were exceptional. They never canceled a lesson or failed to do the assigned work. And within ten weeks, they'd transformed Cinder into a highly focused, high-energy dog, who took direction adoringly from her owners as if they were her salvation.

You can get the same results with your dog.

Some people begin training hoping to transform a "bad seed" into a canine who's as good as their "precious pooch." Pam talked about bringing her adolescent Golden Retriever to my class. "Henry is so naughty compared to Mandy at this age," she said, as if Mandy had been blessed with an obedient personality and Henry was cursed with an obstinate nature. After completing a course, however, Pam sang a different tune. She couldn't stop talking about Mandy's cavalier attitude and young Henry's willingness to obey. Comparisons and feelings of disenchantment are normal when you own two dogs. If troubling feelings interfere with your relationships with your dogs, take the quickest route to happiness and resolution: formal training—for *both* of them!

It's Never too Late . . . nor too Early to Start

Your dog begins learning the instant you bring him home, so if you can, start teaching him good behavior. But, don't despair if you've had your dog for a while; it's never too late to start training. In fact, dogs from 6 to 14 years of age regularly start training programs and make great progress.

Candy was a 12-year-old Lhasa Apso who'd spent her life charging every neighborhood dog that she saw, always from the safety of a leash or a fenced-in yard. Her owner, Janie, assumed that it was probably too late to do anything about the Lhasa, but because she was taking her middle-aged Poodle to training class, she decided to bring the old girl along.

It worked. Thanks to Janie's commitment, Candy began obeying her commands. She was soon under control even off-leash, and her lifelong aggression abated. When the Lhasa died of old age four years later, the loss was tough on Janie—not just because she'd given the dog a home for so many years, but also because, through training, they'd developed a unique bond.

At the other extreme, some of my students bring their dogs into puppy class at 8 weeks of age to learn house manners and simple commands, and return for basic training at 16 weeks of age. By the time these young-sters are 6 months old, they've learned mannerly behavior, all the basic commands *and* off-lead control. Owners are awed that even at this young age, the pups can be so responsive, sociable and readily controllable. Although you mustn't be overconfident—adolescent dogs need to be watched carefully and need periodic, systematic reinforcement—youngsters can be taught to be delightful companions.

A corollary: Don't assume unruliness is a stage that the dog will "grow out of." Allowing disobedience during puppyhood could result in death. With so many pups who haven't had a good start, there aren't enough second, third or fourth homes for them. The tragedy is that over 99 percent of them are perfectly trainable.

Seize the Moment

Anytime is a great time to start training, and today is definitely better than tomorrow. However, certain events offer exceptionally good opportunities for changing a dog's behavior.

For example, relocating provides a great chance to start anew. If your dog has no code of behavior established for his new environment, it's easy to stop problems before they become habits. Whether you made the move with him or are just introducing him to your household, watch him carefully. Be ready to stop his first attempts to jump on the counter, lunge at the window or sniff at the garbage container so that he realizes only penalties, not payoffs. Although bad behavior may occur early on, most dogs tend to be on their best behavior for the first two weeks in a new place; so, supervise him constantly for the first month or two.

Another good time to begin training is after your dog has had surgery. He'll be a bit disoriented from spending time away from home and receiving anesthesia and, depending on the procedure, may be a little sore. Prevent or correct his attempts at mischief-making while he is recovering and then begin obedience training as soon as your veterinarian permits; your dog will welcome the work after the stress of surgery and displacement.

A new home can provide you and your dog with a new beginning in behavior modification.

Designate a Trainer

In many families, all the members want to participate in training the dog—initially. But what starts out as everyone's job quickly becomes no one's. And without proficiency or consistency, dogs can't learn. The results include frustration on the part of the owner and confused canines who are usually, and unfairly, labeled disobedient.

If everyone in the home truly wants to train and is willing to devote twenty minutes for daily practice (which means actually working with the dog, not just walking around killing time), someone in the family should nonetheless act as the primary trainer. Any additional work the family wants to perform under the guidance of the primary trainer is encouraged.

Once you've trained your dog, remember that he may not listen to everyone. Of course, neither do you. If I see you pulling into the best parking spot at the shopping mall and tell you I want to park there, you would undoubtedly tell me to take a hike. You listen to people who have authority over you—people whom you respect.

Similarly, smart dogs obey those who know:

1. how to give the right commands at the right time in the right tone of voice,
2. what reaction to expect from the dog,
3. how to enforce commands.

Sending the Dog Away for Training

Sending your dog away for training is, in the long run, not advantageous. Professionals can turn out a well-trained dog quickly, but they can't teach your dog to bond with you. The bond is only achieved through your work with your dog (and perhaps when he learns to forgive the mistakes you make in training). Moreover, no matter how well-trained a dog may be, he'll never be "flawless": If you don't train the dog from the start, by the time you notice he is slipping, you are unlikely to know how to remedy the deterioration.

> **TRAINING IN PAIRS**
>
> A trainer or handler's physical limitations may make it impossible for him or her to enforce commands in the traditional method. Handlers who lack mobility or are very small compared to the dog may need help. They can give the commands and praise the dog; meanwhile, another handler waits in the background, ready to enforce difficult commands.

If you don't have time to train your dog in the basics of obedience, you don't have time for a dog. The best shortcut to training is to arrange private lessons with a professional who will show you, step by step, exactly how to train efficiently.

The Pros and Cons of Using Treats

Most trainers want their dogs to obey them out of love rather than because they were beaten or bribed. But,

11

because most dogs love tasty treats, food has long been used as a training aid. There are basically three ways to use food in training:

1. as reinforcement for behaviors offered by the dog (operant conditioning),
2. as a reward for completing an already learned task,
3. as a lure to get the dog to perform a task.

Most dog owners use treats as a lure. Consequently, the dog learns to follow the food without understanding that he is to perform a task on command. He may well learn the task in the absence of food, but not in the absence of the body language that accompanied the offering of the food—if the hand holding the treat is lowered to the floor to get the dog to go down, he will probably go down even though there is no treat in-hand. But if you gave the command without a hand gesture, he would have no understanding. By using a lure—treats combined with body language—the dog will do a lot of tasks quickly. However, he will probably fail to notice the thing you ultimately want him to respond to—*your command.* So, if you decide to train with treats, learn how to enforce your commands without them.

If you would prefer not to use treats, don't. I have never found it necessary to use food to teach a task. In fact, I've preferred to stay away from using treats so I can see when the dog is actually learning commands rather than just performing actions.

Is Your Dog "Bad" . . . or Sick?

Feeling poorly can obviously cause behavioral problems in any dog. For example, if your dog has a bladder infection, even intensive housetraining efforts can't correct a soiling; it's a problem he can't control. If your dog is teething and has no toys to chew, he can hardly be blamed for destroying things in the house.

On the other hand, good behavior isn't attained by just making certain your dog is healthy and well provided for; he needs training as well. But training is hard work, and you want the dog's health in your favor, so be sure to:

1. feed him a premium dry dog food,

2. have regular veterinary checkups and keep his vaccinations current,

3. immediately report any health concerns to your veterinarian.

A puppy who breaks a leg or contracts a serious illness needs special care during recovery. Many owners feel so sorry for dogs in this situation that they continue indulging and protecting them long after the condition has cleared up. By doing so, they are providing the perfect environment to foster any dominance or willfulness on the part of the pet. Though your techniques may need modification during recovery, always stop inappropriate behavior.

Some chronic health problems actually alleviate behavior problems. Dogs lacking in vigor may have a physical defect like hip dysplasia or poor vision that inhibits normal behavior and exploration. The owners may take credit for the stellar behavior because they are unaware of the dog's misfortune. When their next dog arrives and exhibits normal, rambunctious behavior, they're unlikely to be able to control it using the same techniques that had been so successful with the ailing dog.

Physical limitation, sad though it is, can make your job easier from a training standpoint, but all healthy, active dogs can be trained.

A Dog Owner's Rights and Responsibilities

Before you make demands on your dog, pledge to be a good owner. Bad management is a human failing for which dogs pay the price. The dog who isn't housed or supervised properly can escape or be teased or injured. Behavioral problems can result from neglect, as well as from abuse. Promise yourself that you will provide your dog with good medical care, sufficient exercise, proper grooming and good nutrition. Because dogs can't express their needs in words, we must observe them and properly attend to these needs. Being a responsible dog owner is not as difficult or mysterious as it sounds.

YOUR RESPONSIBILITIES

Veterinary Care   Keep your dog up-to-date on his vaccinations and free of internal and external parasites. Take him in for regular checkups and heed your veterinarian's advise on precautionary health care such as testing for heartworm and administering preventative medication.

Vigorous exercise is a must for most dogs.

Diet   Your dog's mind and body will be optimally cooperative only when you steer clear of table scraps, treats, food coloring, sugar, fillers and unnecessary preservatives. Cherish your dog, don't destroy, debilitate or indulge him. Simply feed him a high-quality food, recommended by your breeder, a veterinarian or a pet shop, and nothing else.

Exercise   Some individual dogs don't need much exercise. These rare dogs are content with periodic walks and leisurely outings to relieve themselves. But athletic dogs need daily vigorous exercise to relieve pent-up energy. For these dogs, a stroll around the block is just a level above sleeping. A half-hour of constant swimming, running or retrieving is necessary.

Exert your dog by jogging with him, tossing a ball down a hill or letting him play exuberantly with another dog. Of course, don't let him get overheated or dehydrated in the process; unless the weather is cool, exercise him in a shady area and offer him water as needed.

If you have a bicycle, consider buying a stabilizing metal arm that attaches to the bike frame; these attachments (common brand names are the Springer and the K-9 Cruiser) are available by mail order or through a pet shop. Clip your dog's collar to the attachment to keep both of your hands free to steer.

Grooming Good ear, mouth, nail and coat care is usually easy to maintain with a weekly once over. Depending on your dog's breed and the expertise required, it only takes fifteen minutes to two hours to clean his ears, brush his teeth, cut his nails and brush his coat. There's no excuse to neglect this area of your dog's health. If you can't attend to it yourself because of a lack of time or knowledge, there are plenty of qualified groomers who charge very reasonable fees. Besides making your dog feel spiffy, proper, regular grooming will enhance your bond with your dog.

If you leave your dog outside, make sure that he has a place to stay dry and protected.

Housing Safe, comfortable shelter made just for your dog is a necessity. It's no fun for you or your dog to wonder if everything will be okay when he is alone. If you must leave your dog outside, make sure the area is a comfortable temperature, dry, protected from the wind and escape-proof. You want to be confident he'll be there when you return and that he isn't freezing, damp or sweltering. If he's inside, you'll want to be sure that he's not chewing on furniture or cords or soiling the house. At the very least, your dog should have a crate he is accustomed to staying in whenever necessary or a room in which he can be left without doing anything destructive.

Obeying Local Laws Most communities have leash, licensing, housing and vaccination laws that dog owners must obey. Contact your municipal and state governments for copies of the domestic animal ordinances, and make sure that you're in compliance.

15

Being a Good Neighbor   Clean up after your dog. Be mindful of the rights of non-dog owners by keeping your dog quiet, controlled and unobtrusive.

Providing Adequate Protection   Protect him from potential harm, especially when you doubt your ability to watch or to control him or the people or things around him.

Socializing Your Dog   Socialize him so that he is confident and self-reliant when necessary—for example, in the presence of children and loud noises.

YOUR RIGHTS

Your dog may be your buddy, but he isn't your equal. He needs fun, but he must obey rules to exist happily in this society. He needs to be protected but not isolated. He needs to be well-cared for but not spoiled. In addition to responsibilities, level-headed dog lovers have the right to do the following:

Take the Dog Out   Exercise with your dog in public areas on leash.

Have Fun   Play with your dog and embrace the joys of ownership.

Be the Boss   Being a kind pet owner does not mean that you should cave in to a dog's dominant demands. Accustom him to things he may not like (for example, taking pills, bathing, being left alone) for his own well-being just as you would diaper even the fussiest baby.

Be Confident

It's likely that you have doubts about how your training will work out. What if your dog doesn't like it? What if he doesn't respond? What if you don't understand how to do it?

My successful students have one thing in common: Those who follow a plan get results. That doesn't mean that they don't make mistakes, complain that their dogs are arrogant or get frustrated with their occasional human ineptness. It means that they have the courage to keep training. That courage and effort are rewarded with richer understanding and communication between them and their dogs.

I've been training dogs for twenty-two years. I don't want to make mistakes when training, but sometimes I do. If I attempt to train, I may make a mistake—but if I never try, I'll never have the dog I really want. My dog will make mistakes, too. Many of his mistakes are my fault; others are an inevitable, and natural, part of the learning process. It is my responsibility to my dog to hang in there with him. While he is making those mistakes, he may actually be just about to understand what I want. If I quit when he is on the verge of a breakthrough, I've deprived him.

Some owners embark on a training program with tremendous optimism. When progress is slow or nonexistent, however, too many abandon their original goals and settle for meager results. Shoddy, half-learned obedience is likely to deteriorate into annoying behavior problems. Sometimes these owners decide to give training another try—often approaching it with far greater determination and achieving far better results.

Whether this is your first time around or your last-ditch effort, recognize that a degree of frustration is part of the learning process. When in doubt, just keep working with your dog. You may be right on the edge of a learning breakthrough. Don't let your frustration or doubt win out!

A final word of advice: Don't expect to find any shortcuts. Once you've learned the basic training principles, you still have to practice—first, to learn the motions and exercises proficiently and then to do them with your dog over and over again until he learns it. The only shortcut is in finding an effective method, and sticking with it.

chapter 2

The **Right** **Equipment**

A good trainer will start with the right equipment. You'll need the following items, described in some detail below:

1. a well-fitted collar,
2. a 6-foot leather leash,
3. a 15-foot longe line,
4. a tab—a short nylon rope,
5. a 50-foot light line.

Collars

Your dog should always wear a buckle-type collar, flat or rolled, with identification tags. Remove it only when she's kenneled or when she is left alone and you're concerned that it could get hooked on something and strangle her. Remember, though, that if she then gets loose, she won't be wearing the most visible form of identification.

When you begin training, use the collar your dog wears around the house. If she doesn't wear a collar, start with a snugly-fit, buckle collar. Consider switching to a slip collar, a prong collar or a head halter only if you've tried the procedures outlined in this book, doing the exercises correctly and devoting enough time to them, and still have little control over your dog.

SLIP CHAIN COLLARS

When using a slip chain collar, most trainers, myself included, prefer the quick slide and release action of a slip chain with flat, small links. It should be only ½ inch to 2 inches larger than the thickest part of your dog's skull. Although collars this small can be difficult to slide on and off, snug collars deliver timelier corrections. They also stay in place better when positioned high on the neck, just behind the ears, with the rings just under the dog's right ear.

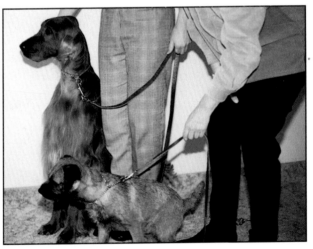

Note the right way and the wrong way to put on a slip chain collar: The Border Terrier's collar is on backward—notice how the chain pulls from the bottom. The Irish Setter's collar is on correctly.

To ensure that the slip collar will loosen after corrections, make sure the active ring (the ring that is attached to the leash) comes across the top of the right side of your dog's neck.

NYLON SLIP COLLARS

Although round and flat nylon slip collars tend not to release quickly, they do deliver stronger corrections than buckle collars. As with any collar, the nylon slip should only be tightened momentarily while correcting. Constant tension around the dog's neck prevents the dog from understanding when she's doing well and when she's doing poorly, because the pressure is always the same.

If using a prong collar, put it on by opening it up, putting it around the dog's neck and then fitting the prongs back into the holes.

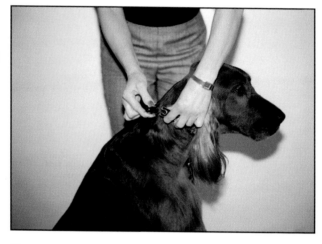

Prong Collars

Prong or pinch collars are useful for dogs who are strong or easily distracted. The prongs come in four sizes—micro, small, medium and large. You can adjust the length by removing or adding prongs. But beware: My experience has been that on occasion, these collars will fall off without warning! For added safety, when you'll be working in open areas, consider fitting your dog with a buckle or slip collar in addition to the prong, and attach your leash to both.

To some people, prong collars look like instruments of torture. They might be surprised to learn some harsh trainers abhor them and some soft trainers embrace them. If you're turned off by the appearance of the prong collar, look for another tool to aid you. If you want to use one, have an experienced trainer show you how to properly fit and work with it. Keep in mind that cruelty or kindness isn't linked to whether a dog wears a prong collar, but rather to the training tactics employed.

Preventing Collar "Escapes"

Your first line of defense against your dog backing out and escaping from her collar is by using the right one—for example, if you work her on a buckle collar, use a sturdy one that won't fall off. Even then, there are no guarantees if your dog has developed this dangerous and naughty habit. Try using the double collar trick. Have her wear both a buckle collar and a slip chain and snap your leash to both collars. When she backs out of the buckle collar, the slip chain will tighten. This not only prevents her escape, it also teaches her to go with the flow instead of fighting you.

The Final Word About Collars

If you use a different collar for training other than the one your dog usually wears, don't expect her to obey well when she isn't wearing her training collar. Be prepared to enforce your commands at all times. She'll soon learn to take you seriously regardless of which collar she's wearing.

These Flat-Coated Retrievers model leashes—a buckle collar and 6-foot leather leash (left), a slip chain collar and 15-foot longe line (center) and a prong collar, tab and light line (right).

Leashes and Lines

Select a leash or line wide enough to control your dog; the larger and stronger she is, the wider it should be. And never let her put the leash or line in her mouth.

Although this behavior may seem charming, it is also the way she'll intentionally distract herself from your training efforts.

THE LEASH

A 6-foot leather leash is used to teach commands and mannerly walking. Generally, for dogs up to 15 pounds, use a leash that is $\frac{1}{4}$ inch in width; for dogs 16 to 45 pounds, use a leash that is $\frac{1}{2}$ inch in width; for dogs 46 to 75 pounds, use a leash that is $\frac{3}{4}$ inch in width; and for dogs over 76 pounds, use a leash that is 1 inch in width.

THE LONGE LINE

A longe line is a 15-foot nylon cord used for many exercises described later, including sneakaway and advanced distance stays, as well as to enforce obedience in spacious enclosed areas like a house or fenced yard.

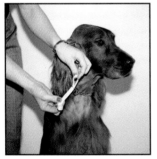

Because many pet stores don't carry them, you may want to go to a hardware store and buy a swivel snap and 15 feet of nylon cord—$\frac{1}{4}$ inch in diameter for a medium-size dog and $\frac{1}{8}$ inch smaller or larger for small and large dogs, respectively. Tie the snap on one end and make a loop for your thumb on the other.

Attaching the tab. Put the loop through the collar.

THE TAB

The tab is a piece of nylon rope, $\frac{1}{4}$ inch in diameter and approximately 18 inches long. If your dog is tiny or giant, adjust the length and width. Tie the ends of the rope together, then slip the unknotted end through the ring of the collar and, finally, thread the knot through the loop. The knot will prevent your hand from slipping off the tab as you give a jerk to enforce commands. However, when you're not holding it, it will be dangling on your dog's chest, which means she is

Put the knot through the loop.

likely to mouth it—rendering it unavailable for you. If she takes it in her mouth, tell her to "Drop it." If necessary, enforce your command by saturating the tab with a chewing deterrent spray or giving your dog a cuff under the jaw.

THE LIGHT LINE AND GLOVE

The light line is a 50-foot nylon cord. I suggest using parachute cord for large dogs, venetian blind cord for medium or small dogs and nylon twine for tiny breeds. The light line is tied to the tab and used as you make the transition to off-lead work.

When you're working with the tab and light line, wear a form-fitted gardening glove to ensure a better grip and to prevent rope burn.

The Retractable Lead

Features   These popular leads come in lengths from 8 to 32 feet. The buttons on the easy-to-grip plastic handle allow you to lock it at a length as short as 4 inches for some models, or as long as the total length or any length in between. You can also let the dog venture away and explore without getting her legs entangled, thanks to a constant, slight amount of tension. This flexibility sounds great, but unknowingly owners using retractable leads are teaching their dogs sloppy behavior. Letting your dog dart and crisscross your path can put you in danger and make you look foolish, while telling the dog that she's in charge. The retractable lead, however, isn't at fault: The user is.

> ### A TRAINING AID FOR SOLVING PROBLEMS
>
> In addition to the necessary items mentioned in this chapter, you may want to have Bitter Apple spray on hand. This harmless spray, which is quite distasteful to dogs, will act as notice that the behavior you are getting is not acceptable to you.

Uses   If you are going to use a retractable lead, use it properly. To make your dog adapt to your pace and stay by your side, lock the lead in the shortest position. When you arrive at the dog's potty area or meet up with a canine playmate, unlock the lead and, with your permission, let the dog pull out the length.

Training

part two

Fundamentals

chapter 3

Basic
Skills

Wouldn't it be great if you could give your dog a training pill or medicine so that he would be a willing, capable student? Before trying to teach your dog to respond to commands, you need to ensure that your dog will respond to you.

The Sneakaway

I use the "sneakaway" exercise to develop my relationship with a dog. Although the sneakaway is an exercise and not a pill, it is the next best thing to a magic potion.

This mesmerizing exercise teaches your dog to be controlled and attentive despite distractions. Use the sneakaway as the foundation for teaching commands and solving problems and to teach your dog to walk nicely on lead. Even without specifically addressing problem

26

behaviors, you may find they magically disappear as your dog learns his sneakaway lessons. At the very least, you'll find that sneakaways improve his general trainability and therefore greatly reduce your workload.

Sneakaways teach your dog that when he is attached to a line that you're holding, he is expected to control himself even though he isn't under command. This lesson in self-control is the foundation that makes other aspects of dog training—problem solving, command training and off-lead control—easy.

Sneakaways: Longe line sneakaway. Hold the handle of the line and run away when the dog is distracted.

THE WALKING SNEAKAWAY

To begin the sneakaway, put your dog on the longe line (the 15-foot nylon cord described in chapter 2), and take him to an obstruction-free area of at least 50 feet square. Put your thumb through the loop of the line and your other hand under it. Plant both hands on your midsection to avoid moving them and jerking your dog. He may get jerked during this exercise, but it won't be because of your hand movement.

As you stroll with your dog, watch him closely but inconspicuously. If he becomes distracted or unaware of you, immediately turn and directly walk in the opposite direction. The line will tighten abruptly if he isn't following as you move away.

The sneakaway is eminently simple: When your dog goes north you go south. When he is thinking of things in the west, you head east.

Practice walking and sneaking away over a two-day period for about one hour total. At this point, your dog should be

Leash length sneakaway. Hold the leash handle and slack in the right hand at your right hip and keep the left hand off the leash. When the dog is unaware or forging, drop the slack, do a right about-turn and run.

keeping his legs tangle-free, be aware of your movements and be willing to be near you.

Although atypical, some dogs, even after an hour of practice, may refuse to budge. Others may throw their paws over the longe line and shake their heads furiously or bite the line. In either situation, you may be tempted to stop momentarily, coax, carry your dog or quit. Resist the temptations—those actions just encourage the behavior and add to your dog's confusion. Instead, create an "umbilical cord" for your dog by tying his leash to your belt. For two days, make him walk by your side as you perform your daily activities around the house and yard. After a few hours of umbilical cording, staying near you should be second nature. Now practice sneakaways again, using a slip chain or prong collar. If you do so for a total of three hours over the course of a week, he is likely to be transformed into a happy follower.

> ## LEASH-BREAKING FOR PUPPIES (AND DOGS OF ALL AGES)
>
> Although you can use the walking sneakaway to leash-break, most people accustom an untrained puppy or dog to the leash prior to training. Put a buckle-type collar and any type of leash on your dog. For ten to thirty minutes, three times a day for a week, watch him drag it around the house or yard. Better still, attach the leash prior to playtime with another dog or toy. He'll step on it, scratch his neck, refuse to move or maybe even scream, all of which you should ignore. Because many dogs like to chew the leash, you may need to thoroughly spray it before each session with a chewing deterrent like Bitter Apple.

As a result of panic or feigned helplessness, a rare dog may jump, spin and severely entangle himself in the line. Ignore his self-created dilemma and refuse to rescue him.

After two or three days you will never see the behavior again. Vivacious types may body slam or nip at you for amusement. With Bitter Apple in hand, silently reel in the line quickly and smoothly, grip the back of his neck (lifting two front feet slightly off the ground), press the Bitter Apple bottle nozzle against the corner of his lip and spray.

THE RUNNING SNEAKAWAY

Use the running sneakaway to help enhance your dog's willingness to focus solely on you. Instead of walking away, pivot and run when your dog's attention wanders from you. Once he's begun running after you, stop dead. At this point, you should take an inventory of your dog's personality, desires and fascinations. He may be intrigued by certain noises, smells, activities, food, toys, new environments, other animals or people. Dog trainers refer to the above items as distractions. Each time you practice, run a little faster as you sneakaway and use more challenging and irresistible distractions.

Stand still or amble if the dog is aware of your intentions. Though you pretend to be entirely relaxed, mentally be ready to sneakaway fast if your dog gets bored and turns his attention elsewhere.

Using Sneakaways with Leash Walking

Once your dog is content to be near you no matter what distractions are around, you can effectively teach him to walk on a loose leash at your left side. Attach the 6-foot leash to his collar and put your right thumb in the handle. Enclose your fingers around the straps of the handle below. Hold the midsection of the leash with your right hand, too, so your left hand is free. The leash should have just enough slack to touch the middle of your left thigh when your right hand is at your hip. If you are very tall and your dog is short, the leash will hang lower on your leg—in the opposite situation (you are short and your dog is tall), the leash will hang closer to your hip.

Correcting Pulling

If your dog forges ahead, open and close your hand to release the slack, then grip the handle as you pivot and run away. Do this when the dog's shoulder is only inches ahead of your leg, rather than waiting until he is tugging at the end of the leash or lunging frantically ahead. When your dog is running after you, pick up the slack in the leash again and stop dead.

Some dogs will run up after a sneakaway, and right past you again. If this happens, pivot once again and sneakaway before the dog bolts ahead. If your dog is a charger, watch his body language closely—you will learn to anticipate when to do multiple, direction-changing sneakaways.

Correcting Lagging and Crossing Behind

If your dog attempts to lag, tighten the leash a bit. Reduce the slack in the leash about 1 to 5 inches as you briskly walk forward. The dog may bump into the back of your legs for the next few steps but that, along with the fact that the leash tightens against your left thigh with every step, will encourage him to return to your left side. Remember to keep your left hand off the leash so nothing interferes with your thigh pulling into the leash.

If your dog wants to lag, jump into the leash.

Correcting Sniffing or Continued Lagging

If your dog is off in scent-land or continues to lag, "puddle jump" with your left leg so he will be jerked back to your left side. As you walk, take a large step with your right foot and instead of taking a standard-size step with your left, take a leap like you were clearing a little puddle with your left leg leading. The smaller and more gentle the dog, the less distance you'll need to cover in your jump.

KEY SNEAKAWAY POINTS

When practicing sneakaways, remember the following important tips:

1. Steady your hands; don't use arm movements to jerk your dog.
2. Move at a constant rate until your dog is following you, then stop dead.
3. Don't allow your dog to hear you move or stop or see you with his peripheral vision. Avoid tricks like scuffing your feet, or inching, bowing or arcing away; instead, always sneak directly away, with conviction, so your dog will learn to pay attention to you rather than your tricks.
4. Be silent. Praise isn't helpful; in fact, it's often detrimental on sneakaways. If your dog is responding so well that you feel inclined to praise him, you may be ready to skip ahead to Chapter 4, "Commands"—but before doing that, read on.
5. To use momentum to your advantage, begin heading away from the dog while there is still generous slack in the line. Time your departure so you'll be able to take two running steps *before* the line tightens.
6. When your dog is doing brilliantly, avoiding jerks no matter how cleverly you attempt to sneakaway, start teaching the tasks and commands described in the following chapters.

GRADUATION EXERCISE

A walk in the park: Take your dog to a new, distraction-filled area. Put him on his longe line, holding just the handle, and take a walk. If his interest begins wandering, sneakaway fast. Continue taking him to new areas several times a week for twenty-minute walks until he's willing to walk on a loose line, aware of your movements for the entire walk.

SNEAKAWAY SUMMARY

Objective To maintain control, attention and a slack leash around any distraction, as a foundation for all other training.

Procedure Hold a 15-foot nylon longe line with the right thumb through the loop and all the slack dragging.

Days 1 and 2 Walk silently and quickly away from the dog when he is inattentive or attempts to wander more than 5 feet from you.

Days 3 and 4 Reinforce the lessons of days 1 and 2:

1. run away when the dog is inattentive or wanders,

2. use distractions,

3. stop dead when line goes slack.

Days 5 and 6 Continue to reinforce by making the exercise more challenging:

1. run as fast as you can when you sneakaway,

2. use more tempting distractions,

3. train in different locations.

Using Distractions in Training

Distractions are one of the most important tools used in training your dog to obey. If Rick had nothing better to do, why wouldn't he obey? But Rick's priorities change with his environment. If food is being prepared, leaves are blowing around, people are laughing and talking, or cats, rabbits or birds are present, Rick may forget all about obedience in his excitement. Fear can also cause Rick to tune you out; running from the killer vacuum, savage lawn mower or spooky garbage can is likely to render all your obedience training useless until you've used plenty of distractions in conjunction with these exercises.

Practice daily around distractions—you want your dog's attention on you!

THE BENEFITS OF ACCUSTOMING YOUR DOG TO DISTRACTIONS

Obedience is needed desperately in times of emergency. Suppose Rick spies a vicious looking stray dog in your neighborhood. To avoid getting attacked, it is crucial that he promptly obeys your Come and Sit and Stay commands. Then you'll be able take action to stop the stray dog's advance and protect your own dog.

Practice daily around temptations and insist that your dog give you his undivided attention so you can gain control anytime you need to, regardless of what he wants to do. Using distractions will separate the trick dog from the trained dog. When your dog's well-being is at stake, which do you want?

KEEP DISTRACTIONS INTERESTING

In every training session, use both old distractions that still fascinate your dog as well as new temptations. Your dog's reliability will develop by repeatedly distracting him, then correcting him in the recommended manner.

There are an abundance of distractions available. Try placing soup bones in your training area. When you're done, put them in the refrigerator until your next session. When your dog accompanies you on your errands, do a five-minute lesson in a new area. Use your imagination when working with distractions in your training, and your dog will reward you for your efforts.

chapter 4

Commands

The commands you use to elicit action from your dog should be clear, concise and consistent. But don't feel obligated to use a customary or standard command like Heel if you'd prefer to use a word like Side. In fact, perhaps you don't want to use words at all. A snap of your fingers followed by a point to the ground could mean lie down; in fact that will come in handy when you are talking on the phone and you want your dog to stop misbehaving. Whistles are also great attention-getters. Associations between behaviors and whistles are easily formed.

Hand signals are among the least practical form of communication. In order to see the hand signal, the dog must give you his undivided attention. If you already have your dog's undivided attention, how much more control do you need? I love teaching hand signals and although they are impressive, they're not imperative.

Seeing Results

Everyone asks, "How long does it take to train a dog?" Unlike the question, "How long does it take to get to Atlanta?" dog training is an intangible process, not a concrete one with an absolute destination. The answer depends not only on the dog and the trainer, but also on what the dog needs to learn to be considered "trained." What constitutes a trained dog varies depending on who you ask. The average person can expect to achieve excellent understanding and response from his dog after twenty or twenty-five minutes of daily practice for ten weeks. But every person's idea of training, and how vigorously to work at it, varies. The previous estimate is based on the assumption that the trainer works his dog like a driver drives a car—with full concentration, eyes on the road and never taking for granted the competence or awareness of other drivers or pedestrians. The most successful dog trainers react instantly and appropriately to their dogs, are adaptable and undiscouraged by detours and don't linger at intersections but eagerly keep driving toward their destinations.

Dog training instructors often have students who, against recommendations, only train their dogs once a week in class. Some of these dogs respond reasonably well in class. I've seen a response in my own young, untrained demonstration dogs. After only about two or three demonstrations, they no longer respond like untrained dogs; even after a tiny bit of work, they attain a minimal understanding of the exercises during class or demonstrations. But they can't be considered trained. Real learning means that the dog will perform the appropriate response on the first command, amidst any distraction without any physical encouragement like being touched or jerked.

Some dogs are very responsive to formal training.

Dogs, like people, have different aptitudes. Some people have a knack for language, not science, and some dogs have a knack for stays, not recalls. Some dogs respond to formal training like some people respond to traditional schooling; easily and naturally. Formal training is recommended for all dogs and is most beneficial for those confounded by it. Dogs do learn how to learn, so that after ten weeks, it becomes difficult to separate the "naturals" from the initially confused or resistant.

Avoid Breed Stereotyping

Prevent myths from becoming self-fulfilling prophecies.

No breed has a patent on problems or virtues, and stereotyping breeds does more harm than good. Just like people, all dogs should be evaluated on their individual temperaments and characteristics.

I once owned two Australian Cattle Dogs. One was far more similar in temperament to my tough and independent Standard Longhaired Dachshund than to the other cattle dog—a mild and gentle-natured soul. You *should* heed warnings to be extra conscientious of certain breed tendencies. For example, be aware that a sporting dog in a heavily scented field has a strong desire to follow her nose, rather than listen to you; be ready to intervene when a terrier breed exhibits aggressive tendencies toward other dogs; and be prepared to spend a good deal of time socializing herding breeds.

Praise

Parents, bosses and dog trainers must give praise at the right time in the right way. Kids, employees and dogs need it as confirmation that their actions are correct. The best trainers inject words of it during work to acknowledge and congratulate specific actions, concentration and worthy intent.

Praise is to dog training what humor is to life—it makes difficult times endurable and good times joyous. Use it in response to your dog's effort, and your enthusiasm will grow with hers. Keep in mind, however, that when it comes to humor, what charms one may well repulse another. The same is true with praise: You will have to experiment with a variety of ploys to find what delights your dog no matter what her mood. I've found quiet, interesting sounds, combined with scampering movement, gentle pushes and vigorous, light, brief scratching with my nails usually elicit a good response. Whatever you use, your dog's reaction is the most important indicator that you are on track. Does your type of praise make her eyes bright and get that tail wagging? If she is bored by your technique, improve your delivery or revamp your routine.

Praise your dog in a way that she likes.

Never praise your dog if she does her work in a distracted or preoccupied manner; she may think you are praising her inattention. Instead, do sneakaways to help her realign her priorities.

Rules for Teaching Any Behavior

When teaching any particular behavior, the rules are the same:

1. Decide on your cue (a specific word command, finger snap and signal, whistle or hand signal used every time, but only for that particular behavior).

2. Decide on how to elicit the desired behavior (enforce the Sit, for example, by pulling up on the collar and pushing downward on the dog's rear).

3. Give the cue as you elicit the desired behavior (to simplify descriptions, the remaining chapters will refer only to verbal commands, but feel free to substitute whistles, finger snaps or signals, if you prefer, while following the same plan).

Twelve Basics for All Commands

1. Define your intent. What do you expect the dog to do?

2. Define the cue. What clear visual or auditory signal will you use to initiate the desired action?

3. Use the cue while you appear confident yet pleasant.

4. Preface verbal commands with the dog's name. The name and command should sound like one word ("Betsy, Heel," rather than "Betsy . . . Heel"). The only exception to this rule is when giving the Stay command, since this tells the dog not to move.

5. Say the command only once, so your dog learns to listen to every command.

6. Instill an association between the command and the conduct. While teaching, give the command as you make the dog do the action (for example, say Sit as you pull up on the collar and push down on the dog's rear).

7. Give commands only when you can enforce them so you don't risk teaching disobedience.

8. Decide on reinforcement. How are you going to show the dog what to do? Unlike the other eleven steps, this will change depending on your dog's stage in training.

9. Show appreciation with praise. As you see your dog learning, "Good, good, good!" should become a reflex.

10. Release the dog from every command with a chin touch and the word Okay.

11. Test your dog's understanding. Before progressing to the next level, make sure your dog can work around distractions.

12. Never take obedience for granted. Dogs forget, get lazy, become distracted and inevitably fail to respond to familiar commands. Correct your dog so that she understands that the rules haven't changed and neither should her behavior—especially if she rarely makes a mistake.

The Release

You need two cues, one to begin an action and one to end it. Release your dog from duty with a word like Okay or Free. Pair this word with an outward stroke under the dog's chin. Dogs who rely on a physical release cue are less inclined to "break" their commands. For the first three weeks of training, step forward when you deliver the Chin Touch–Okay to make the dog move off the command on cue.

Recommended Daily Warm-up

RUNNING SNEAKAWAYS

Practice a few running sneakaways until the dog is following you attentively regardless of distractions.

LEASH LENGTH SNEAKAWAYS

Leash Grip   Hold the leash by placing your right thumb through the loop of the leash. Put slack in the right hand, too.

Remove the left hand from the leash and walk with the dog at your left side.

Procedure   Drop slack and run to correct forging. Walk briskly ahead to correct lagging and crossing behind.

Stationary Commands

SIT-STAY

Step One: Sit

a) To teach the Sit command, put your dog on your left side, hold the collar with your right hand and put your left hand on her loin just in front of her hip bones and behind her rib cage. Command Sit as you pull upward on the collar and push downward on the loin. If she is rigid and won't budge, move her forward and walk her into the Sit. Some dogs will turn their heads to mouth or bite you or roll over on their backs. Keep a firm grip on the collar and firmness in your wrist as you pull her up into the Sit. Once she is facing forward with her front paws on the ground, loosen your grip. Steady the slumping or mouthy dog by continuing to grip the collar and giving a series of quick, light up and down jerks. Your collar-holding hand should move in a cadence similar to a fast rap on the door (knock knock knock), so her front paws gently bounce on the ground a few times.

SIT-STAY AT A GLANCE

1. Sit command (three steps)

   a. Pull up/push down

   b. Jerk up/push down

   c. Piston jerk/no push

2. Sit-Stay (one step away)

3. Leash Length Sit-Stay

4. Distance Sit-Stay

5. Out of Sight Sit-Stay

Demand a quick Sit by jerking up as you take your final step.

Talk, pet and praise, but don't let the dog move. Keep pushing her back into the Sit as you tighten up on the collar. After a few seconds, release with a Chin Touch–Okay.

b) After three days with no sign of resistance, command Sit, and wait for a response. To reinforce your command, push downward on the loin and give a quick upward jerk on the lead.

c) Eliminate the push and just use a sharp, split second jerk-and-release action. If after two jerks she doesn't sit, use a jerk and push combination. Emphasize the jerk and use the most minimal push possible. Many dogs find it rewarding to be touched, whether you are petting them or pushing them into the Sit. Therefore, to teach a reliable Sit on command without a push, jerk to provide an incentive.

When giving a jerk, start with a belly of slack in the leash and with your hands gripped about 5 inches from the snap.

Graduation Exercise Sit your dog on a strange-feeling surface—plastic bubble wrap, gravel or a wire grate. If she refuses, place her in the Sit, and try a more neutral surface like wet black top, slippery linoleum or sand. Then command her to sit on something really comfortable like a thick rug, plush carpeting or a pillow. Several times a day practice the Sit on the most difficult surfaces first, then practice on a neutral surface and finally a comfortable surface. Consider the command mastered when she willingly obeys the first Sit command on the strangest surface.

Regardless of the direction of the jerk, the collar should tighten for only a split second.

Immediately return your hands to the starting position.

Step Two: Sit-Stay One Step Away

Prerequisite Your dog will sit on command and wait to be released with Chin Touch–Okay.

Procedure Hold the leash taut over the dog's head. Command Stay, step in front of her and act busy while producing distractions. Return to praise frequently and, finally, release with Chin Touch–Okay. Moving the head and wagging the tail is acceptable, but you should correct scooting forward, rotating and attempts to

41

The Sit-Stay: Teach your dog to sit in the presence of distractions.

Enforce the Sit with a two-handed jerk.

Command Stay.

Remain one step away and test your dog with distractions.

stand with an upward jerk. If one jerk doesn't stop it, the jerk was too slow or light. If two stronger, faster jerks don't work, use a jerk and push combination. Some dogs respond well to two or three light jerks given in quick succession.

If your dog tries to lie down, tighten the leash enough to prevent her from lowering comfortably into the Down position and give her praise as she realizes she doesn't have enough slack to lie down. Loosen the leash and prepare to repeat this sequence many times during the next week of training if your dog is inclined to recline.

You may be wondering why you should care about lying down on the Sit-Stay if you're not working toward obedience or field competition. The answer is simple: You need your dog to sit, not lie down, so you can look in her mouth, administer medication or ear ointment or wipe dirt off her paws. Say what you mean and mean what you say to avoid confusion in all areas of training.

Troubleshooting Tip Quickly and silently jerk and push to prevent or stop movement.

Step Three: Leash Length Sit-Stay

Procedure Command Stay and walk out to the end of the leash, holding its handle. Use distractions like stepping side to side, bending down, pulling forward lightly on the leash or dropping food or toys in front of your dog. This teaches her that no matter what your preoccupation or what activities surround her, she is to stay put. Frequently tell her that she is good.

Stop movement immediately by:

1. sliding your free hand down almost to the snap of the leash as you step into your dog,

2. quickly maneuvering your dog back into place without saying a word,

3. jerking upward,

4. moving back to the end of the leash.

Slide down the leash as you step in and jerk upward to correct movement.

Step Four: Distance Sit-Stay

The objective is to free your hands and allow you to go farther away without the risk of your dog running off.

Prerequisite Your dog Stays with extreme distractions when you are a leash-length away.

Procedure

1. Tie your longe line to a stationary object.

2. Heel your dog to the snap of the longe line so she sits facing away from where it is tied.

3. Snap the longe line to the collar (leaving the leash attached to the collar, too). Command Stay and walk away.

If your dog bolts, she'll be jerked by the tied line. To stop any undesirable movement, run back and use a two-handed grip on the leash (near the snap) to move the dog back to the area, then into the Sit position with a jerk.

THE ART OF THE JERK

1. Get a grip on it; a short grip on the leash that is. When jerking, your hands should be no more than 8 inches from the snap of the leash so you can give a timely, directional jerk of the proper strength.

2. Where's your belly? The leash should maintain a belly of slack (be free of tautness and tension) before and after the jerk. It only tightens for the split-second jerk.

3. A proper jerk is a two-handed job; unless your other hand is busy placing your dog or carrying your pooper scooper. By using a two-handed jerk, you'll have better control of the speed, direction and strength of your jerk. Two-handed jerks ensure accuracy, which is especially important when training little dogs who need only a featherweight correction.

Step Five: Out of Sight Sit-Stay

Your dog learns to remember your instructions even when you are invisible.

Prerequisite   Your dog Stays with extreme distractions even when you're far away (see "Distance Sit-Stay").

Procedure   Sit your dog behind a corner and step out of sight while still holding the leash. Throw distractions into her view.

Troubleshooting Tip   If she moves, correct her quickly by sliding your hand down the leash toward her collar and then giving an upward jerk. Quickly move out of sight again after giving the correction.

When increasing distance on the Sit-Stay, do it safely.

Graduation Exercise   Enforce Sit-Stays while you:

dress in the morning

vacuum

make a salad

clean your car

carry groceries

open mail

greet the mail carrier

make a phone call

shop in a busy
pet store

When you no longer need to allow spare time for corrections, your dog has mastered the Sit-Stay.

General Rules for Stays

Use the following training guidelines to make sure that your dog masters the Stay.

1. Just before leaving your dog, use a hand signal along with your Stay command. To signal, flash the palm of your free hand, fingers down toward her eyes.

2. Use distractions—movement, food, toys, people, places—to make sure she's learning.

3. Pay attention, and move in to correct the instant your dog begins leaving the Stay position; otherwise, she won't know what the correction was for.

4. Correct silently. The more you repeat commands, the more your dog will learn to ignore them. If your dog didn't listen the first time, let your hands and leash do the talking.

5. Adapt the strength of your correction to your dog's size, level of training, why she moved and how excited or distracted she is. When an appropriate correction is ineffective, it should be strengthened.

6. Leave immediately after the jerk.

7. End all Stays by returning to the dog's right side, giving praise, then releasing with the Chin Touch–Okay.

DOWN

Step One: Down with Push
Objective   To introduce your dog to the Down command.

Procedure   Place your thumb and index finger behind the dog's shoulder blades and on either side of the backbone. Command Down as you push. If the dog braces, use your right hand to pull her head down to the ground as you push. If you simply can't get her down, discontinue work on the Down and concentrate on perfecting the Sit-Stay around distractions; rare is the dog who fights on the Down after becoming completely cooperative on the Sit. Praise by scratching her tummy, and then release her with Chin Touch–Okay.

> **DOWN AT A GLANCE**
>
> 1. Down with push
> 2. Down with push and jerk
> 3. Down with two-handed jerk
> 4. Machine Gun Down

Step Two: Down with Push and Jerk Combination
Objective   Teach your dog to lie down without the two-finger push.

45

Teach your dog to Down by pulling her collar downward as you push her down using your thumb and index finger to apply pressure behind her shoulder blades and along her back bone.

After about one week of practice, enforce the Down using the two-finger push and a quick jerk toward her back toe.

When she is going down easily (and often on command alone), use just a two-handed jerk to enforce.

Procedure Enforce Down by simultaneously using a two-finger push and quick jerk.

Jerk diagonally toward the dog's right rear foot by holding the leash close to the snap while you stand facing the dog's right side.

Step Three: Two-handed Jerk— No Push

Enforce Down by using a two-handed jerk without the push. If two jerks don't work, combine a firm jerk with a very light two-finger push.

Step Four: Machine Gun Down

Objective Get your dog to lie down without a hand signal or touch.

Procedure Practice three one-minute series of Down, Praise, Release exercises in rapid-fire succession. If you are generally doing ten to seventeen downs per minute, you are using the right cadence.

Perfecting the Down

Exceptional dogs may learn the verbal Down command in a week. With an average of twenty repetitions per day, most dogs will lie down 50 percent of the time after one month.

But getting certain dogs into the Down can look like a scene from all-star wrestling. It's better to deal with these shenanigans in your house than at the veterinarian's office, where similar protests will be common if you haven't done this homework to abolish tantrums.

Many dogs try to weasel out of the Down with their paws and mouth. Though they aren't actively threatening, the owner may be advised to wear a sweatshirt, pants and gloves so flailing nails and teeth can't scratch the skin. Three ten-minute sessions practicing Down, Release, Down, Release, over and over usually teaches compliance. Have one hand on the collar pulling downward and the other on the pressure point behind the shoulder blades.

Avoid pointing and bending when you give the Down command.

Menacing protests call for more practice with sneakaways and the Sit. Teach an instant response around any distraction with a gentle Sit command and preface Down practice with leash-length sneakaways in a highly distracting environment. When the dog is giving her attention to you instead of the temptations, she is likely to cooperate on the Down as well. Also, instead of drilling Down after Down, only do two or three at a time. Practice another exercise, do a couple

Stand still and upright when giving your Down command.

Downs, and repeat the pattern so during each session twenty or thirty Downs are practiced.

Graduation Exercise   Command Down with your hands in your pockets. Eliminate using body language by standing in front of a mirror. Your mouth is the only part of your anatomy that should move when commanding Down.

Give the Down in a whispering tone.

Turn your back and look over your shoulder at your dog to give the command.

Try it when lying on a bed, floor or couch, sitting in a recliner and standing in front of an open refrigerator.

DOWN-STAY

Objective   Teach your dog to lie down and stay for grooming and examinations or for long periods— during meals, for example, when the dog is just too frisky.

Prerequisite   Your dog will sit and stay on command around distractions and will lie down on command.

Procedure   Down your dog and command Stay. Examine her ears, eyes, teeth and paws. Use the jerk alone or the combination jerk and two-finger push to correct movements like crawling, rolling or ascension. Correct grass munching, sniffing or biting (herself or you) by grabbing the back of her neck and giving a closed fist cuff under her jaw (see leash biting correction, chapter 2).

Praise her frequently when she cooperates, and return to her right side to praise and then release her with the Chin Touch–Okay.

Progression   Follow the same progression described in Sit-Stay:

1. Down-Stay One Step Away
2. Leash Length Down-Stay
3. Distance Down-Stay, (Tied)
4. Out of Sight Down-Stay

Moving Sit and Down (five steps)

1. Command Sit, pivot, jerk up
2. Command Down, pivot, jerk down
3. Command while walking
4. Command while running
5. Command out of the blue

    a. In house

    b. In yard

    c. During play

Objective   Teach your dog to sit or to lie down while moving and from a distance.

Prerequisite   Reliable Sit and Down at your side around distractions.

Procedure:
Step One   Walk forward with your dog on Okay release. Command Sit as you pivot to face her and jerk up simultaneously. Say "Good dog!" as you back away.

Step Two   When your dog sits on command without the jerk, command Down as you pivot and jerk downward. Back away and praise.

Step Three   When your dog will stop and position herself on command, say Sit or Down as you look over your shoulder and continue walking. Run back to her to correct if she doesn't stop dead.

Step Four   When your dog will position herself on your command as you continue walking, give the Sit or Down command when you are running together.

Troubleshooting Tip   If your dog is having difficulty with the Down, perfect the procedure using the Sit command. Then try practicing Down again.

Step Five   When your dog least expects it, give a Sit or Down command. Start when you are in the house and your dog is meandering around. When she has mastered that, practice Sit and Down outside. Eventually your dog should sit or lie down on command, even during play.

After one month of consistent practice, most dogs will sit or lie down on command 90 percent of the time during play. Correct slow responses to the Sit or Down by rushing back to your dog's collar, moving her back to the spot and jerking her into position. If the Sit and Down-Stay are weak, this weakness will magnify, so review Sit and Down-Stay as needed.

General Rules

1. If your dog doesn't stop dead on command:

   a. Run back to correct her, and

   b. Use the same leash correction you use for breaking a Sit or Down-Stay.

2. Praise her verbally for compliance.

3. Return to release with the Chin Touch–Okay.

STAND-STAY

Step One: Stand

Objective   Teach your dog to Stand from a sitting position and not to move until she's released.

Procedure Begin with your dog sitting. Hold the collar so the knuckles of your right hand rest against the dog's chest. Run your left hand along either side of the dog's body, to the front of the rear leg along the stifle (knee), as you command Stand. Push backward gently on the dog's stifle and forward on the collar if the dog doesn't stand on her own. Say "Good dog" as she begins to stand. Take your hand off the stifle and start petting her. Continue holding the collar and praising her until you release her with a gentle push to the side and "Okay."

To teach the Stand command, hold the collar and touch the dog's stifle to stand your dog or to stop movement.

Troubleshooting If your dog is submissive, fidgety or sensitive about handling, don't despair. Put a leash or piece of rope under the girth of the submissive dog who thinks she should sit when you hover over her. Simply command Stand as you lift the rope. Loosen the tension when she stands, but prepare to tighten it again if she doesn't stay standing. For a restless or sensitive dog, Heel her along a wall, command Stand as you pull forward on the leash and touch her stifles with a yardstick to prevent unnecessary movement.

Step Two: Stand-Stay

Objective Your dog will stay standing while the handler circles and examines her.

Prerequisite Your dog stands without resistance and remains in place for thirty seconds until released. The dog should also know the Sit-Stay.

Procedure Stand your dog, command Stay and begin circling your dog. Keep one hand on the collar and use the other to stroke her head, feet and body. If the dog tries to move her feet, stop her by using a horizontal jerk opposite the movement. Accompany the jerk with a light touch on her stifle with your free hand so she cannot sit as you correct her. Release her with a gentle push to the side as you command Okay. Gradually increase the length of the Stand, beginning with ten seconds and working up to one or two minutes. Most dogs will do a one-minute stand after two weeks of practice.

Perfecting the Stand

Exceptional dogs will do a one-minute Stand-Stay for examination in the first session. However, some dogs will need weeks or months of daily practice. This should consist of sitting for thorough examinations by strangers, as well as separate practice with brief Stand-Stays. Eventually they will understand Stand-Stay means to pretend to be a statue.

Troubleshooting Tip When practicing the Stand, give all leash corrections in a horizontal direction while you're standing by the dog. Never jerk upward, downward or from a distance because, in dog language, an upward jerk means Sit, a downward jerk means Down, and a jerk from a distance means Come forward.

Moving Commands

HEEL (THREE STEPS)

1. Position and procedure
2. Automatic Sit
3. Perfecting Heel position with turns

The Heel command teaches the dog to walk on your left side regardless of your pace or direction and to sit when you stop. Gone are the days of your dog pulling ahead or dragging behind, weaving from side to side or getting underfoot during walks. As the dog learns to heel and you learn how to teach her to move precisely, a deeper learning takes place for both of you. The dog's awareness, watchfulness and willingness grow as she learns to remain in position. Because you need to watch your dog very intently during the process, you'll develop an ability to anticipate your dog's next move— otherwise known as reading your dog.

Heeling: Move the collar high on the dog's neck so that the rings of the collar (any type) are positioned under the dog's ear.

In the correct Heel position, the dog's shoulder will be aligned with the handler's shoulder on the handler's left side.

Command Heel as you begin walking forward.

When you halt, command Sit, as you pull up the lead and push down the dog's rear.

Trust and respect develop as you and your canine partner master the art of heeling. This newly formed bond will help you channel the dog's energy more efficiently no matter what the task, challenge or obstacle.

Step One: Heeling

Objective   To teach your dog to maintain Heel position on your left side, with her shoulder aligned with yours and her body 3 inches from your leg. The position is the same whether you're moving forward, turning or stationary. When you stop, your dog should sit automatically.

Prerequisite   Practice of sneakaways (steps one through three) for at least one week, until dog is attentive to you despite distractions.

Procedure   Hold the leash in your right hand with your right thumb through the loop and four fingers holding the slack just as you did during leash-length sneakaways. Command "Betsy, Heel" as you begin walking. Prepare to stop by grabbing the collar with your right hand and using your left to place her rear end into a sitting position so her right front foot is alongside your left ankle.

As you walk along preparing to halt, it's easy to grab the collar with your right hand if you use the fold-over maneuver. Grab the leash with your left hand and hold it taut over the dog's head as your right hand grips the braiding or stitching of the leash just above the snap. Take your left hand off the leash and use it to place the dog in a Sit in perfect Heel position as you stop.

Troubleshooting Tip If your dog forges ahead, do a Leash-Length Sneakaway. Drop the slack of the leash, grip the handle, hold hands at your waistline and run away. As the dog returns to your side, return to the original leash grip, holding the slack, as you continue walking. If your dog lags behind, say "Good dog!" as you spring ahead by taking a puddle jump with your left leg first. As you do this, your left thigh will pull the leash, and your dog, back to Heel position. The jump ahead will also prevent the dog from crossing behind to the right side.

Prevent your dog from sitting askew by swinging the rear straight with your left hand before she sits.

Step Two: Automatic Sit During Heeling

Prerequisite Your dog will sit 80 percent of the time on command, as you stop, without needing to be touched or told.

After a week or two of practice, or when the dog sits without resistance, use a two-handed jerk as you stop to encourage a straight, fast Sit.

Procedure Warm up by gathering the leash in both hands and giving a light upward jerk as your finish your last step. After two or three halts and good attention from your dog, halt and gather the leash. Jerk only if the dog doesn't stop in Heel position and sit immediately.

To stop forging or lunging, sneakaway.

Step Three: Perfecting Heel Position with Turns

Objective To stop tendencies to heel too far from or too close to you, and to correct slight forging and sniffing of the ground by using sharp left and right turns.

Procedure Use the "Jackie Gleason Left Turn" to stop slight forging, crowding and sniffing of the ground: Turn 90

To stop crowding or minor forging, turn left and shuffle into the dog until she nestles back into the Heel position.

degrees to the left, then step perpendicularly into your dog so your left foot and leg slide, or step behind her front legs. Shuffle into her until she becomes attentive and moves back to the left side. Practice slowing your pace abruptly, then turn left immediately if your dog's shoulder is even 1 inch ahead of yours. If your dog attempts to cross in front of you to the right side, tighten the leash with your left hand as you continue to step into her.

To stop wideness, sniffing or lagging, follow a right turn with a puddle jump. Pivot 90 degrees to your right on your left foot, take a large step in your new direction with the right foot and leap forward with your left leg as if you were jumping over a puddle. As you jump the puddle you should feel the leash against your left thigh, pulling the dog forward. Steady your leash by holding your right hand against your right hip as you leap.

Jump and praise simultaneously to motivate your dog. Hold the leash in your right hand so the slack will remain in front of your thighs as you jump.

COME

There are two types of Come commands, also known as recalls: those that are obeyed and those that are ignored. The latter type costs a lot of dogs their lives. The former type can give you an ego boost you'll never forget. When I think about outstanding recalls, two instantly come to mind.

The first one occurred when I was walking my notoriously untrustworthy husky off-lead in a field. Suddenly, she bolted off toward the local pond. First, I felt frustrated: After all these months of training she can't be trusted to stay around. Then, I felt hopeless: There she goes, running full boar and I am powerless over her. Finally, I got mad. She was more than half a football field away when I cupped my hands around my mouth and screamed "Tess, Come!" That day I made two major errors. The first was taking her off-lead when she wasn't ready to be off-lead. While she did listen sometimes, especially in class, she wasn't reliable at times like this.

The second error involved giving commands she would probably disobey. Then, in disgust, I'd say "See how disobedient she is?" The dog was wrong, but I was right.

Despite anything I did wrong or didn't do right, Tess ran a few strides more, then miraculously spun around and was now running full boar toward me! You'd think that in my jubilation I would be yelling "Good, Girl! Atta Girl!" But no, not me. Everything about my training was atrocious up to that point, why change now? Stone-faced, I watched her complete the recall, told her it was about time and walked her back home.

The other memorable recall occurred when I was giving a lesson on off-lead control to the owners of a Beagle and a Basset Hound. The owners' expansive property had trails, woods, fields and ponds. For this private lesson, I had brought several of my own dogs to act as distractions, but I found it wasn't necessary. There were lots of scents and animals around. The owners, frustrated that they had this great place but couldn't let the dogs run and enjoy it, were ready to concede defeat, haplessly declaring "hounds will be hounds."

> **THE COME AND FRONT COMMANDS AT A GLANCE**
>
> 1. Come
>   a. Reel
>   b. Pass the Puppy
>   c. Jerk
>   d. In Pursuit with Leash
>   e. Distance
>   f. In Pursuit with Light Line
> 2. Front
>   a. Reel
>   b. Pass the Puppy
>   c. Jerk
>   d. In Pursuit with Leash
>   e. Distance
>   f. In Pursuit with Light Line

"It's just a matter of proper training," I said just as my Whippet spied a bunny and zipped off in pursuit. I interrupted our conversation with "Orbit, Come. Good girl" and turned back to look at them and smile at their open-mouthed expressions after I kneeled down to greet Orbit.

Thereafter they viewed their dogs' potential with more optimism but no more commitment. Sadly, the dogs listened to me but not to them. Their goals were realistic, had they followed through and enforced their commands.

The day I became a better trainer was the day I realized the most predictable thing about dogs is that they are not infallible and that I need to take precautions.

Step One: Reel

Procedure   Leash your dog and take her for a walk. If she begins sniffing something, gazing around or meandering off, call "Betsy, Come!" Immediately back up quickly as you reel the leash, praising enthusiastically. Kneel down when the dog arrives, using verbal praise only. Release with Chin Touch–Okay and continue practicing the sequence.

Troubleshooting Tips for All Recalls   Some dogs will come but stay out of reach or dart right past you. Some owners, without realizing it, encourage the dog to cut her approach and stay farther away by attempting to cradle, caress or hug the dog. Petting the dog as she arrives can create or worsen these recall problems because extending your arms makes it appear that you are protecting the space in front of you. Keep your hands to yourself to avoid putting a recall barrier between you and your dog. Don't pat the dog—it will discourage her from coming close. Use verbal praise to acknowledge, encourage and congratulate the dog's arrival. Practice us-ing verbal praise as your dog is approaching because unlike physical praise, you can use it from a football field away.

Step Two: Pass the Puppy

Get your family to join the program by leashing the pup when at least one other member is present. Have one person hold the leash while the other holds the dog. When the person holding the leash handle calls "Betsy, Come," the other lets go so the pup can be reeled in as the trainer of the moment backs up. Then the people should switch roles. This exercise can be practiced daily for up to fifteen minutes; if you and other family members habitually use the same consistent training techniques, the dog will learn to respond to everyone in the family.

*Come command: 1) Command Come, reel dog in, back up, praise.
2) Use distractions and enforce command with jerk. 3) Teach dog
to come when she is in pursuit. 4) Put dog on light line for distance recall with distractions. 5–7) Enforce distance Come, pick up
line, wrap around palm and run away while praising. 8–10) Before reducing length of light line, practice off-leash type corrections;
walk to dog, jerk her toward you, continue to back up and praise
so that she runs toward you on her own. 11) Greet dog's arrival
every recall, squat down to give verbal praise, do not touch dog.
12) Release dog with Chin Touch–Okay. 13) Follow same steps
to teach Front command, but insist that dog sit squarely in front.*

Step Three: Jerk

Procedure   After twenty step-one recalls, your dog is probably running toward you faster than you can reel. Now see if she'll leave distractions when you stand still and call Come. If she doesn't respond promptly, use a piston-type horizontal jerk toward you as you praise and back up. The jerk emphatically tells the dog "wake up and do it on your own." If she did respond to your command, praise and back up. When your dog responds to your command around strong distractions 80 percent of the time, proceed to step four.

Step Four: In Pursuit with Leash

Objective   To teach your dog to stop and come when called, even if she's running away or you're following her.

Procedure   Three times this week create a situation that would cause your dog to forget her training and pull toward a distraction. For example, arrange for a friend to ring your doorbell. Fifteen minutes before the designated time, leash your dog and relax in a chair positioned at least 20 feet from the arrival door. When the dog hears your visitor and jumps out to investigate, follow and call "Betsy, Come." Jerk the leash and back up if the dog doesn't respond to your command. If she does respond, praise and crouch down and then release her with Chin Touch–Okay.

Step Five: Distance
(wear a glove when using line)

Prerequisite   On-leash, your dog will come on the first command; on a slack leash, your dog will come on the first command around any distraction.

Procedure   Attach a long, lightweight line to your dog's collar. When she's distracted, position yourself over the line and call her. Praise her during the entire recall, from the time she begins taking her first step toward you until you release with Chin Touch–Okay. As she arrives, squat down and release with the Chin Touch–Okay.

If the dog ignores your command, correct her by grabbing the line and using Wrap, Run and Praise—wrap the line around your hand twice just above where your thumb attaches to your hand, make a fist around the line and anchor your hand on your waist as you run away from your dog, praising all the way. After you feel the line jerk, drop it, face your dog and crouch down with your hands behind your back as you keep praising. Release with the Chin Touch–Okay.

Step Six:
In Pursuit with Light Line

Objective   To teach your dog to stop her pursuit and come back if you call.

Procedure   Go to an area where your dog would like to venture out and explore. Wear a glove and have your dog drag the light line. Do the Wrap, Run and Praise with a slight variation: As she is moving toward a destination or following a scent, pick up the line, wrap it around your hand, anchor your hand to your waist and start running. Time your command so the line tightens to jerk her a split second after she hears the command.

Surprise Party Recalls

This special assignment teaches reliability in real-life situations. The Come command is traditionally taught by telling the dog to Sit and Stay, then walking away and calling her to Come. People wonder why the dog does so well in class but poorly at home and when playing. The training situation (in which your dog is poised and totally controlled in Stay, intently watching you walk away) in no way resembles a situation in daily living (in which a dog examining rabbit droppings is entranced by the activity and oblivious to you). Recall work targets breaking the dog's focus from distractions when she hears the Come command; but she must also respond to unanticipated commands when she isn't in "practice."

Try explaining to a rabbit who runs in front of a truck with your dog following, "Give me a chance to practice a warm-up recall." Most trained dogs obey reliably after one or two corrections. But that isn't a real-world luxury. Whether her last recall was a minute ago or a week ago, this next exercise will teach her to come instantly, every time (well that's an exaggeration—she is a living, breathing companion who is entitled to make a proportionate number of errors just like her owner).

Prerequisite Your dog is controlled around distractions when she isn't under command because 1) you NEVER allow your dog to pull and 2) you've practiced in-pursuit recalls.

Procedure Twice weekly for thirty minutes, take your dog to a new location, one she will eagerly explore and continually investigate. Try parks, fields, a friend's yard or anywhere you can enforce your command properly. Attach a very long (50 to 200 foot) light line to her collar and allow her to roam. Put on your gloves and every five minutes or so, when she least expects it and is running away, call and Wrap, Run and Praise.

Taking the recall one step further could save your dog's life as it did that of a Dachshund I owned. In her previous home, the Come command was often repeated but rarely obeyed. I began teaching the Come exactly as outlined in this book. I also began the Front command. Not only was the Front more demanding than Come, but it was also more effective because it had never been disobeyed. One evening I was walking three of my dogs to the car after training classes. Their leashes dragged on the ground as I reached for my keys with one hand and struggled to maintain my grip on the training equipment with the other. Just as we approached the car, a rabbit darted out in front of us and the dachsie took off. I called "GoGo Front!" and she stopped dead, turned around and walked back. Had I called Come she likely would have kept running just like she was used to doing in her other home. When I called Front, GoGo bet that I was ready to reinforce it. She also probably suspected that I had put the rabbit there as a test. It was 10pm, half a block from a busy city intersection. Had she not turned around immediately, I might never have seen the little dog alive again.

FRONT

Objective   Front means to come briskly and sit facing you with paws in front of your feet until released with the Chin Touch–Okay. In this position the dog will be close enough for you to easily touch her.

Procedure   Call Front, then back up as you praise and reel in the leash. Grab the collar with one hand and place the dog's rear end straight with the front end as she arrives in front of you. Release with a Chin Touch–Okay. Repeat this exercise at least ten times per day for a week.

After one week, most dogs require only gentle guidance to sit; after four weeks, they should be sitting automatically. When the dog usually sits automatically but forgets if she is distracted, enforce the position with a jerk up as you use your other hand to control the straightness of the rear.

Some dogs will vigorously fight your attempts to precisely position them in the Sit. Calmly hold the collar and firmly reposition the struggling dog no matter how much she flails, twists or attempts to turn. With your hands still on her collar and rear, tell her that she is good when she settles down and then release with the Chin Touch–Okay.

> ### SUMMARY OF RECALL RULES FOR THE COME AND FRONT COMMANDS
>
> 1. Don't practice cross-your-fingers obedience by giving commands your dog may not obey and you know you can't enforce.
>
> 2. Formalize your voice, always using the same enthusiastic tone which suggests urgency, to say "Betsy, Come!"
>
> 3. Move away after calling to appeal to your dog's desire to chase and help ensure a faster recall.
>
> 4. Use verbal praise only; don't pet the dog, because it will repel her. Be especially enthusiastic in your praise as she approaches—don't wait until she arrives or your apparent lack of commitment will reduce her commitment to the process, too.
>
> 5. Squat to acknowledge recall finale—her final approach and arrival.
>
> 6. Go opposite to correct. If you suspect the dog isn't going to make a direct approach, quickly move away from the dog's line of movement so she gets jerked toward you.
>
> 7. Release immediately with a Chin Touch–Okay to reward a good response.

Follow steps two through six as described for the Come command but substitute the Front command and

Before you try heeling off-leash, see if your dog can maintain the Heel position when the leash is out of sight. Hold the leash behind your back in your right hand.

Enforce the automatic Sit with a two-handed upward jerk.

Pat your leg to encourage the lagging dog.

To correct lagging or walking on your right side, grab the leash with your left hand and position it on your inner thigh, then jump ahead.

make the dog sit squarely in front of you until you release her with the Chin Touch-Okay.

Off-Leash Commands— Bridge that Gap

The concept of off-leash training is a bit of a misnomer. All teaching is done on-leash. If the dog isn't fully prepared on-leash, her lack of understanding will magnify when the leash comes off. Off-leash work only reinforces the good work she does on-leash.

Is your dog really ready?

Before attempting off-leash work, try this experiment: Think of the worst temptation for your dog—guests, children or other dogs—and arrange to test your dog's readiness for off-leash work around those temptations. With your dog dragging her leash, and your arms folded or in your pockets, give a Sit, Down or Come comand in a nonthreatening tone of voice. Try this test in the house around guests or in a pet shop that allows canine customers. Praise her if she listens, but pick up the leash if she doesn't. If she is now pulling on the leash, sneakaway. If she stands by you as you picked up the leash, fold your arms, leave the leash totally slack and give a single command to sit. If she obeys, read on. If she doesn't, review sneakaways and basic on-leash commands around distractions before returning to this section.

HEELING WITH LEASH BEHIND BACK

Objective Prepare your dog for off-leash control by teaching her to maintain her position regardless of where the leash is.

Procedure Hold the slack (but not dragging) leash in your right hand, behind your back. Correct forging by turning left. Encourage the apprehensive or lagging dog by patting your thigh and gently jumping ahead without tightening the leash. If she continues meandering away from the Heel position, grab the leash with your left hand, place it inside your left thigh and jump ahead while praising.

Turn left if your dog tries to forge ahead.

After three weeks of solid practice, most dogs will walk in Heel position on your left side regardless of your speed and direction and sit automatically around distractions. Exceptional dogs will do it in three sessions. Distractible, lazy, apprehensive or young dogs under 5 months of age need a special approach. Keep off-leash practice brief, and attempt it only after a daily warm-up of sneakaways around distractions. To ensure your dog's willingness, follow sneakaways with brisk on-leash heeling with lots of corrections on halts, changes of pace and turns.

STRAIGHT JACKET COMMANDS

Have you ever waved back at someone only to realize that the person was actually greeting someone behind you?

Dogs make incorrect assumptions just like we do. And we often make erroneous assumptions about a dog's understanding, especially in the case of off-leash control. Simply removing a leash changes your posture, which can confuse a dog. On-leash, some people consciously or unconsciously use excessive body language and gestures, which, when the dog gets farther away during off-leash work, no longer seem significant. The act of obeying a simple Down command may have been based more on your posture, body language and gestures. When you give the command without those aids, your dog probably won't understand it. If, when you remove the leash, she doesn't obey, it could be because she never really learned to obey the command in the first place. The next exercise will get your dog used to obeying the new you.

Procedure   Attach the leash, fold your arms or put your hands in your pockets, and give Sit, Down, Stand, Stay, Come and Front commands. Use just your voice, no gestures. After all, if your dog is running away all she'll hear is your voice, and the gestures will be wasted.

To enforce these "straight jacket" commands, avoid touching the leash. Instead, walk to her collar to make an "off-leash–type correction." Reach for her collar and jerk upward to enforce Sit, jerk down to enforce Down and jerk her forward toward you as you back up to enforce the recall commands. If she tries to dodge you as you reach for her, replace the leash with a longer line. This will allow you to walk right up to her by stepping on the line. Be calm and confident. Practice around distractions, day after day, until, in the rare event she disobeys, your dog doesn't dodge you as you reach for her collar to correct her.

Closing the Gap

To make the transition to off-leash control, you'll need to use a light line (discussed earlier) and a tab (described in chapter 2).

Objective   Your dog demonstrates her readiness for off-leash obedience, while you maintain your ability to correct her.

Prerequisite   Your dog has mastered leash-behind-the-back heeling and straight jacket commands.

Procedure   Tie a long, light-weight line to the tab and let your dog drag it as you practice commands. Only touch the line and tab when correcting. Control your dog with commands. If she disobeys and runs off, step on the line, then walk along it until you can give her collar the appropriate corrective jerk.

HEELING

Confidently command Heel as you move out briskly. Pat your leg or puddle jump with praise to encourage a reluctant or lazy dog. Use lots of turns, halts and speed changes to keep her focused. Quickly move in the opposite direction if she leaves the Heel position, and praise her as she returns. Note: Before attempting a 180-degree pivot during heeling, perfect your U-turns and 90-degree right turns.

If she doesn't return, correct her by using the Wrap, Run and Praise: Walk to your dog and reach for her tab, slide your hand from the tab down the line a few feet and twirl it around your hand, put your hand on the inner thigh of your left leg and puddle jump or run ahead as you praise. Drop the line and continue heeling after this correction.

If your dog is still hesitant, call Come and run 20 feet. Squat to praise her and resume heeling practice when, three times in a row, she runs happily by your side. If she won't budge on the Come command, walk to the tab and give it a horizontal jerk with praise as you run to the destination. If she still won't move, practice calling Come and running with the line in hand for the remainder of the session.

> ## LIGHT LINE PARTICULARS
>
> 1. Because it's made of nylon, a light line is both easy to handle and durable.
>
> 2. Choose a test weight that is strong enough to hold your dog in the smallest diameter possible.
>
> 3. Make sure that the line is long enough that you feel confident to let it drag on the ground, knowing that if you need to correct, you will be able to reach it before your dog is out of range. A length of 50 to 100 feet should be enough for any dog who has had the advised prerequisite training.
>
> Remember, the only time you touch the light line is to either step on it or grab it to stop your dog from running away.
>
> Gradually shorten the line's length to wean your dog off the line

If your dog begins forging, stop immediately and enforce the automatic Sit or turn left into her to cut her off.

SIT, DOWN, STAY, COME AND FRONT

Practice these commands, correcting errors by jerking with the tab, the same way you did on the leash.

STAND

Correct errors by jerking the tab in the direction opposite the dog's movement as you touch the stifle (knee). Continue standing your dog by touching the stifle just as you did when teaching step one. Unlike the other commands, which you give at a distance or when you're indisposed, the Stand is used exclusively when you are next to your dog and fully attentive. Therefore, there is no practical reason to teach response to a verbal Stand command.

Weaning Your Dog Off the Light Line

If your dog is off-leash and isn't listening to you, you can try to bribe her with a ride in the car, plead with her, play hard to get and run away, flatter her with praise or coax her with a treat. All of these ploys are designed to get your dog back to you and permit you to attach a leash, but none reinforces your command. The one way to do that is to walk to her, grab her collar and correct her. However, most dogs won't let you approach them. The real meaning of off-leash control lies not in the dog's ability to obey commands, but in your ability to approach her without her running away. No matter how well trained she may be, no dog is ever perfect; she will make occasional mistakes. Before going naked (completely off-line), make certain your dog will always allow you to approach her. Praise her for letting you approach her before you enforce the command. Attempt this step only when your dog no longer tries to dodge her responsibilities—or you.

Objective   To achieve total off-leash control.

Prerequisite   1) Your dog usually obeys commands around distractions, 2) she needs no warm-up to remind her of her responsibilities and 3) she accepts impending corrections without thinking about running away.

Procedure   Cut off 20 percent of the light line every three to seven days if you've tested your dog around distractions. After one month of practice with the line dragging, you should feel confident to begin weaning the dog off-line by beginning the cutting process. If your dog has a perpetual "spring fever" attitude, superior on-leash control will be necessary before beginning the weaning process, and a greater number of daily practice sessions around distractions will be necessary as you reduce the length of the light line.

Other Important Commands
WAIT (FIVE STEPS)

1. Wait at Door
2. Wait at Door with Distractions
3. Cross-Through
4. Out of Sight
5. Wait in Open Areas

What command should you use when you want your dog to stay in the car, stay back from the doorway, stay out of your way or stay in the kitchen? The Stay command probably seems like the obvious choice to you but will likely confuse your dog. You want the dog to stay in or out of a certain area, but your dog has learned that Stay means to remain in position either sitting, standing or lying down. Certainly you could use the Stay command as a door opens, but that is ridiculously restrictive if you are leaving for work. Wait is a better solution; it means "Don't go through the door," not "Freeze until I return home." It tells your dog not to leave an area but allows her to move freely within that area.

To understand the difference between Stay and Wait, think of what you would expect if you told a child to stay sitting in his high chair in contrast to if you asked him to wait in his room. Sitting in the high chair is good, but twisting around in the chair, dancing on the tray or lying on his stomach with his feet kicking is not. Playing a game or engaging in an activity within the room is fine, but standing catatonic at the doorway is unnecessary. Also, Wait, like Stay, has nothing to do with duration. It lasts until the next direction is given, twenty seconds or twenty minutes later.

Step One: Wait at Door
Teach the Wait command at doorways first. Choose a lightweight door, estimate how wide your dog's front

end is and open the door 2 inches more than that as you command Wait. Stand there with your hand on the knob of the partially open door, ready to gently bump the dog's nose with it should she attempt to pass through the opening. Be sure never to shut the door while correcting. Instead, leave the door open with your hand on the door handle, ready to stop attempted departures with an abrupt and silent bump of the door. If necessary, butt her with a quick movement that makes it appear that the door is snapping at her every time she tries to peer or charge out. The procedure is the same whether the door opens in or out. Practice with lightweight doors until you feel confident that the timing and strength of the tap is appropriate to deter your dog. Leash your dog so that if your attempts to deter her fail and she successfully skips across the border, you can step on the leash and prevent her defection.

Step Two: Wait at Door with Distractions

Practice at familiar and unfamiliar doors as an assistant tries to coerce your dog to leave. Your assistant can talk to the dog and drop food, but he or she shouldn't call your dog. As your assistant remains on the opposite side of the door, engage in lively conversation to teach your dog that even when you are preoccupied, the Wait command is enforced. Then apply the technique at heavy or sliding doors, and finally, without the leash.

If your dog waits but, when released, bounds through the door, say Sit following your Chin Touch–Okay. Have her leashed so that you can insist that she stop dead by using a two-handed upward jerk if necessary. Practice the pattern of Wait, Okay, Sit, Come Inside until she is responding on a slack leash. Command Sit following every invited exit. When she does it on a slack lead the first time through, start doing the same pattern with the leash dragging. If she obeys with the leash dragging, try it on-line and finally off-leash. She should now usually proceed through doorways in a mannerly fashion, but surprise her with that Sit command a few times each week to keep her sharp.

Step Three: Cross-Through

Teach your dog to obey the Wait command as people are passing through the door. After saying Wait and opening the door, hesitate before you or your guests pass through the door. You may need to give a reminding correction to convince her to back off so you can easily pass through. Should she try to slip out as you're in the doorway and are unable to tap her with the door, use your knee to bump her back.

Step Four: Out of Sight

To enforce the Wait from behind a door, begin by commanding Wait at a door that opens out. Stand momentarily with the door open, ready to tap your dog. If she obeys the Wait command, cross through the doorway so you're standing behind the door, hand on knob, completely out of sight. Throw distractions and have children run in and out as you watch, ready to tap her snout with the door should her nose appear in the opening. Now, whether you're present or not, she'll respect your command.

If you want your dog to follow you through the door or to come through after performing the Wait, tell her so by using the Chin Touch–Okay. Whenever the dog is nearby, command Wait or Okay, depending on your intentions when passing through a main doorway.

Most dogs will have a solid grasp of steps one through four above after

---

THE FLYING WAIT

The Flying Wait is designed to heighten your dog's understanding of the Wait command. Attach your longe line to a stationary object, such as a tree or street post. Snap the longe line and the leash to your dog's collar. Hold the leash, begin walking away from the stationary object, command Wait when the line is about to tighten, and keep walking with the leash in hand. If she didn't stop on command, she did when the line tightened, so stand at the end of your leash and praise her. Return to the stationary object and repeat the sequence. If she is stopping on command, try running away instead of walking. Keep attaching the longe line to a new area so that she learns to obey your commands rather than to stop in a certain place.

---

a total of twenty experiences at five different doors. But beware of assuming that your dog understands the Wait if she hasn't made attempts to pass and hasn't gotten bumped: She's likely to make her move when you are most complacent and unprepared.

Step Five: Wait in Open Areas

Once your dog understands Wait at doorways as a result of your door-tapping correction, you can use the Wait command to keep your dog in or out of designated areas, indoors or outside.

BOUNDARY TRAINING

1. Determine the boundary—do you want the dog to stay on a rug or in the kitchen or out of the landscaping? The area should be defined by some type of marker; a change in surface, a dividing rope or anything noticeable that you've laid down.

2. Attach a long, lightweight line to the dog's tab.

3. Command Wait as she is about to enter the off-limits zone.

4. Jerk the line to stop her from entering the off-limits zone.

5. Keep the line "grounded" between corrections. Except for the split second that she's being jerked, the line should be dragging on the ground, out of your hand.

6. Praise her verbally (not physically) if she obeys your Wait command or following a correction. If the dog begins coming toward you, fold your arms, turn your back and ignore her.

Staying in Her Own Area

If you want to leave your dog on a rug or teach her not to follow you into the house, tell her to Wait There as you step off the area. Stay near by, act busy and tempt her with distractions. Tell her to Wait if she tries to leave. Grab her collar to jerk or gently toss her back in the area to correct.

Magic Marker Wait

When a boundary is only periodically enforced, such as insisting that the dog stay out of the kitchen during meal times, consider signifying your expectations with a special marker rather than the Wait command. Place a highly visible rope or cloth on the border of the taboo area and tape it down to secure it. Initially command Wait if she tries to cross, but drop the command after several sessions. Practice by taking the dog to the park and making a giant roped circle around her. Never allow her to cross over the rope, and then remove the rope to signify her freedom.

For magic marker boundaries outdoors, you need a long, lightweight line to attach to your dog's collar and a distinctive marker to designate the area.

OFF: AKA "GET YOUR PAWS OFF AND DON'T JUMP UP"

If you want your dog to stop jumping on people, furniture or counters, you have four ways to enforce the Off command:

1. Knock the dog off-balance with a sharp knee bump to the chest.

2. Jerk the leash opposite to the direction of her jump.

3. Slide your toe sideways under her rear feet.

4. Use your open palm to quickly and lightly tap her nostrils.

Lay down the marker and give the Wait command as your dog attempts to step over the marker.

Especially if your dog jumps on other people or when she isn't close by, always have her leashed so you can deliver timely corrections. Of course, say Off a split second before the correction.

To enforce the Wait command, use the collar to gently toss her back behind the marker.

QUIET

There is nothing wrong with a dog barking if you can silence her easily when necessary. Feel free to praise and encourage your dog for appropriate barking, such as when an intruder is near. Barking is not, however, necessary for a dog's well-being, so if you find any and all barking disturbing or unacceptable, correct it.

To release the dog from the boundary, remove it.

Introductory Technique

Teach the Quiet command by leashing your dog and creating a situation likely to elicit barking—seeing another dog, engaging in ruckus play, being around guests or hearing the telephone ring. Command Quiet when she vocalizes and distract her with a sharp jerk of the leash or a quick spritz of Bitter Apple against her lip as you hold her cheek to ensure an accurate spray. Praise her when she is quiet.

After a half dozen corrections, issue the command and only correct when necessary. If you're commanding from a distance or when your dog is tied outside, kenneled or caged, attach a long leash to her so you can deliver a jerk—from any distance—as she hears Quiet. Though not as timely, you can enforce the Quiet command by running up to spritz and leaving quickly. Some dogs are so pleased you've come back, they continue barking every time you leave despite the correction. That's why corrections given at a distance—whether launching a shaker can (a soda can with eight pennies inside), spraying water or jerking—are preferred.

Troubleshooting Tip   Never threaten your dog with Bitter Apple or a shaker can. Warning her to behave as you expose your ammunition will only teach her to respect the bottle or can. To teach her to respect *you*, wait until she has disobeyed to demonstrate how you intend to respond. Your reinforcements should be kept silent and hidden, before and after use. Moreover, never spray Bitter Apple at your dog. It is to be used as the dog is chewing or barking and the bottle is to be pressed against her lip line before depressing the sprayer. The more you have used Bitter Apple on your dog, the tougher it's going to be to spray quickly and accurately. Keep the Bitter Apple hidden in your hand, ready for use, and before taking the bottle out of hiding, grip your dog's collar with your free hand to ensure better aim.

DROP IT

Some dogs, and virtually all puppies, like to chew, carry and mouth anything they can—hands, clothing, the leash, gravel, cigarette butts, landscaping timbers, tissue. Your first reaction may be to pry her jaws open to remove it, but the tendency to grab the next available object increases if you do. This is because your actions show that you are interested in the object. Either your dog is going to get annoyed that you are stealing her stuff instead of finding your own or, in the case of a more service-oriented dog, she will delight in presenting you with everything she can find and thus save you the bother of picking it up yourself. Therefore, instead of removing an object, teach your dog to Drop It. Drop It can also be used when you want your dog to leave something you anticipate she is about to grab.

Accompany the Drop It command with a sharp jerk of the leash, as you quickly back away and call Front. Then release with the Chin Touch–Okay and offer to play with an acceptable object. If your dog has something in her mouth and your jerk doesn't cause her to drop it, spray your finger with Bitter Apple and touch her gum with the sprayed finger as you issue the Drop It command.

Teach your dog the difference between her toys and taboo items. Place a number of personal items and paper items on the floor and allow the dog to explore. As she picks up a taboo item, command Drop It as you jerk the leash, moving her away from the item and toward the toy. Encourage her to play with the correct item.

Troubleshooting Tip   If the dog doesn't drop a taboo item as you jerk the lead and move away, spray your finger with Bitter Apple and slide your finger along her gum line as you command Drop It. If she still doesn't drop, spray Bitter Apple directly against her lip line.

LEAVE IT

If the dog is about to pick up an item that is not for her, you can either use the Drop It command or introduce a new phrase such as Leave It. In either case, when you notice her eyeballing a taboo item give your command and a quick jerk of the leash as you back away from the item while praising all the way. This looks very similar to step two of the Come command, but use the Drop It or Leave It command when your dog appears covetous.

Sneakaway Exercise to Make Command Training Easier

If you encounter difficulty while teaching any command, sneakaways may be the best way to overcome them. You may be met with resistance or confusion or experience the normal learning curve in which moments of brilliance are peppered with periods of complete ignorance. Rather than calling it quits for the day, increase your chance of turning an unsuccessful day around with these techniques.

When you've met the proper prerequisites, your corrections will be timely and snappy. But if today they don't deter her movement on stays or encourage her to come promptly away from distractions or if she is fighting you on the Stand, Sit or Down, forget about giving commands and work on new and improved sneakaways.

If at First You Don't Succeed . . .

Is your dog still struggling against your attempts for her to sit, down or stand? Do you feel confident that her squirming and resistance are signs of a lack of cooperation? Is it clear that any discomfort she may be experiencing is a result of her antics against your handling and that our introductory technique is being properly done and not unintentionally hurting her? If you answered "yes" to these questions, use sneakaways to settle her down. Leash your dog and do off-the-tail sneakaways with a host of distractions. Drop food, take her to new areas like parks or trails, practice around other animals, domestic and wild. The moment she begins watching you, start working on the Sit, Down and/or Stand. Tell your dog to stay in the presence of these distractions.

If you find the dog is up to the old games of snapping, twisting and so on, do a few more sneakaways and finish with a series of ten Sit commands. Enforce these when necessary with a two-handed upward jerk followed by words of enthusiastic praise and the Chin Touch–Okay. For the next several sessions, practice just the sneakaway and sits. Thereafter, reintroducing Down, Stand, Stay, Come and Front should be no problem.

The
Good
Companion

part three

Guide

chapter 5

Manners

Dogs are opportunists. This doesn't mean they are bad; it just means we are foolish if we walk out of the room leaving goodies on the coffee table and truly believe our dogs would never even think about touching them.

Good Behavior in the Home

Giving a puppy or untrained dog freedom in your house can be deadly. Natural curiosity and boredom cause them to chew electrical cords, ingest toxic substances and destroy valuables. When given freedom too soon, dogs who don't accidentally execute themselves often become homeless because of damage the owner could have and should have prevented.

If you don't know where your dog is, he is probably into something that he shouldn't be. House manners aren't difficult to teach if you always keep tabs on your dog by 1) keeping your eyes glued on him, 2) "umbilical cording" him or 3) confining him to a safe, destruction-proof area. The first option is self-evident . . . but often not practical, given the lifestyle of the average preoccupied dog owner. So let's take a closer look at options 2 and 3.

UMBILICAL CORDING

Many owners think watching their dog means knowing what area of the house he is in. But many forms of

misbehavior can evade this kind of supervision. So if you can't follow him, have him follow you by umbilical cording.

Procedure Tie the dog's leash to your belt on your left side. Give him only enough slack to keep him at your side without your legs becoming entangled. If he attempts to jump up, chew, bark or relieve himself without your approval, you'll be able to stop him instantly by jerking the lead. You'll be able to train your dog as you tinker, work or relax at home. You can even umbilical cord two dogs at once. Or when one pet is trained and the other isn't, you can cord the untrained dog while the giving the reliable one his freedom.

Umbilical cord your dog to teach him proper indoor behavior.

CONFINEMENT

During training, every dog needs a spot where you can put him in which he can do no wrong. When you can't shadow your dog or use the umbilical cord technique, confine him to a place where inappropriate behavior isn't an option. I suggest crating because it eliminates

Crating: Bring your dog to the opening of the crate on leash, then point inside and command him to go inside.

Pull his collar forward as you boost his rear to help him in.

Make him wait briefly as you give a word of praise, keeping one hand on the door ready to bump his nose if he tries to emerge.

Invite him out with a Chin Touch–Okay and repeat the sequence several times daily.

the risk of the dog damaging woodwork, flooring, wall covering or cabinetry.

Especially if your ultimate goal is total freedom, crating is a rearing necessity. Provided the dog is properly introduced as specified below, crating is widely accepted by behaviorists, dog trainers, veterinarians and knowledgeable dog owners as a humane means of confinement. You should feel as comfortable about crating your dog in your absence as you would putting a toddler in a high chair at mealtime.

Whether the enclosure is a room, hallway, kennel or crate, it should be:

1. **The right size.** If your dog soils the area, it's probably too large for him.

2. **Safe.** You would feel awful if your dog poked himself in the eye, stabbed or hung himself or swallowed wood splinters or material like wallpaper or blankets because of confinement; make sure there are no protrusions or sharp edges, and no components that could be ingested.

3. **Dog-proof.** If he is prone to chewing, scratching or jumping up, prevent access to any woodwork, linoleum, furniture, counters, garbage or windows.

INTRODUCING YOUR DOG TO THE CRATE

To accustom your pup to the crate, teach him to go in and out of enclosures on command. Put his paws right in front of the opening. With one hand on his collar and the other pointing into the crate, command Bed. Pull him in by the collar as you place your hand under his tail and behind his rear legs to prevent him from backing away. If necessary, lift him in. Immediately invite him out with the Chin Touch–Okay and try five more quick repetitions.

Practice this routine three times or more every day until he goes to bed on command at least fifteen times a day—*without* being enclosed. If you shut him in and leave him every time he goes to bed he may develop a bad association with crating. But when he learns to go in the crate on command as a result of frequent practice, he is more likely to also accept being enclosed.

Unless he is trying to tell you that he would like to relieve himself, ignore any noise he might make. Most dogs will quiet down if you act oblivious. If yours doesn't and you or your family members are losing sleep or sanity, startle him into being quiet. Try throwing a shaker can at his covered crate, clap your hands sharply twice or anoint him with the spray of a water pistol between the eyes. You can also create an earthquake by attaching the leash to his crate and giving it a jerk as he barks. If he's keeping you awake at night, move the crate close to your bedroom door. This way you won't have to leave your bed to administer a correction. If you're using a leash jerk, attach the handle to your bed post for easy access. Gradually move the crate farther from the bedroom if you desire, as he learns to sleep quietly through the night.

> ## YOUR DOG'S CRATE SHOULD BE HIS HAVEN
>
> Your dog should be comfortable and at ease in his crate. If you reserve his favorite toy for the times he spends in the crate, he may actually look forward to crating as an opportunity to play by himself. Create a peaceful environment by covering the crate with a sheet. Avoid leaving a TV or radio on because your dog may become a victim of unsettling and noisy programs. Replace that cacophony with white noise; the gentle whir of a fan puts dogs at ease.

A crate-trained dog is not housetrained. The crate is nothing more than a place to put your dog when you're unable to watch him. Until his household activity has been monitored hour after hour, month after month, and attempts at naughty behaviors have been curtailed, he is not to be trusted. Therefore much shadowing and umbilical cording will be necessary to teach your dog how to function in the house.

HOUSETRAINING

Housetraining is simply a matter of teaching your dog where you want him to relieve himself (and where you don't). The degree of difficulty depends on your dog and your expectations. Some dogs will never go where you don't want them to, as long as you provide them access to the appropriate place. Unfortunately, most dogs don't housetrain that easily. Even paper trained dogs who always have access to papers or outdoor trained dogs with a doggy door at their disposal may be challenged by the housetraining process.

HOUSETRAINING RULES

Just about any dog *can* be housetrained if you:

1. delay his freedom

2. restrict his diet

3. teach him to eliminate on command

4. take note of his personal habits

5. teach him to find it repulsive to go potty in the wrong place

Procedure

1. If your dog's history is spotty or you're suspicious of his intentions, always supervise, crate or umbilical cord him. Giving a puppy or untrained dog a window of opportunity to use the house as a toilet is asking for trouble.

Giving an untrained puppy the run of the house is courting disaster.

Although your dog may have just relieved himself outdoors, don't assume it's safe to let him roam the house. Sometimes puppies and mature dogs relieve themselves several times in a short period of time for no apparent reason. Even if he isn't inclined to soil indoors, supervision is crucial: It prevents untrained dogs from discovering how to raid the trash container, steal laundry, jump on counters or chew furnishings.

Plan on a year or more to complete the housetraining process. Although your dog may be flawless for days, weeks or months, under certain conditions any dog can backslide. Seemingly benign events such as these can cause housetraining regression:

    a. changes in diet which can disrupt normal elimination patterns,

    b. weather changes (too hot, cold or wet, or noisy thunderstorms) which can make outings unproductive potty times,

    c. new environments (vacation homes, new house or a friend's house) that may be treated as an extension of his potty area rather than his living quarters,

    d. some medications (like allergy medications) and certain conditions (like hormone changes associated with estrus [heat]) that can cause more frequent elimination.

2. Feed a high-quality diet. Buy food made of nutritious, easily digestible ingredients and minimal fillers. You'll pay more, but your dog will eat a bit less and therefore eliminate less. You will find these at pet shops, or your veterinarian may sell them. Ask your breeder or veterinarian to recommend a good diet.

Of course the ultimate test of a good food is how your dog responds to it. He should maintain the proper weight and muscle tone, have a healthy sheen to his coat and have plenty of energy. Gas, loose stools, constipation, itchy skin, bald patches or listlessness indicate a problem that may be diet-related. Consult with your veterinarian to find the proper remedy. If you do switch food, do so gradually over a period of at least five days. Begin with a 20 to 80 ratio of new to familiar foods, and switch the ratios 10 to 20 percent daily to maintain the firmness of his stools.

Avoid giving your dog treats, people food or edible toys like pig ears. Dogs experiencing difficulty with housetraining will achieve control more quickly if they're only fed a single, consistent diet. Additionally, by avoiding treats, people food and edible toys, your dog will be less likely to become overweight or aggressively possessive when food is near.

Don't necessarily put food and water in the crate with your dog when you leave. He will be more likely to soil the area if you do. Besides, most pups will dump the bowls and swim in the food and water, rather than eat and drink.

If your dog doesn't eat within ten minutes of setting the food down, take the food away.

Dogs who eat on a schedule are more likely to relieve themselves at regular, predictable times. Pups should be fed three times a day up to 3 or 4 months of age, and after that can be fed twice daily for the rest of their lives. If your schedule requires you to be gone for six- to eight-hour periods, the amount of food offered need not be the same at each feeding. Consider feeding a larger portion when you will be home for a few hours and will therefore be able to give your dog an opportunity to go out.

If your dog doesn't eat in ten minutes, take the food away. At the next feeding, give the scheduled amount. If you feed a giant portion, you'll encourage erratic eating—starving and then gorging. If your dog regularly refuses to eat, reduce the amount of food by 10 percent weekly until he is eating normally, as long as his weight is adequate. Of course, if he is underweight and refuses to eat, seek veterinary advice. Avoid feeding canned food to coax him into eating. Once he gets a taste of moist food, he may reject dry kibble. This is unfortunate, because canned food is usually less nutritious and much more expensive.

3. Teach your dog to eliminate on command. This trick is handy both when he is distracted and thus uncooperative and for when he's on a surface that he finds uninviting—for example, a kennel run, wet grass or where other dogs have been. Some dogs will only eliminate if they're walked in a particular area. By teaching your dog to eliminate on command, you can get him to go where you want, when you want, and simplify the housetraining process. Here's how to do it.

Leash your dog and take him to the potty area. When he begins the sniffing and circling ritual that immediately precedes elimination, start chanting a phrase like "Potty, Hurry Up." What you say is unimportant, but it should sound melodic and should always be the same phrase. Use the same words for defecation and urination. After a week of chanting during pottying, begin the chant as soon as you enter the potty area.

The purpose of leashing the dog is to enable you to keep your dog moving and sniffing within the appropriate area, and thus speed the process of elimination. If you sense your dog is about to become distracted from his duty of looking for a place to eliminate, use a light quick jerk on the leash as you slowly move about the area yourself.

Give your dog only a few minutes to eliminate. If you give him twenty minutes, he is likely to demand thirty minutes next time. After a few minutes, put him back in his crate long enough to make him thankful for the next potty opportunity you give him.

How often should you take your dog out? When active rather than resting, you will notice a significant increase in the frequency of elimination. At 2 to 4 months of age, most pups need to relieve themselves after waking up, eating, playing, sleeping and drinking—perhaps as often as every thirty to forty-five minutes, depending on the type and amount of activity. At 4 months of age, the dog may be developed like an adult internally, but expect him to behave like a puppy. Most adult dogs can gradually and comfortably adapt to two to four outings per day.

> ## A TRICK OF THE TRADE
>
> If your dog won't relieve himself but you know that he has to, run with him for a few blocks to stimulate his metabolism. If that doesn't work, try the popular trick of dog show exhibitors: Take a whole paper match stick and put just the flint end into the dog's rectum. If your dog has a tail, hold and lift its base while you insert the flint portion of the match stick. If your dog has a nub instead of a tail, you'll hold and lift more skin than tail. Then take him to the potty area and if he needs to use it, he probably will. After a few experiences with the match stick and your chant, your dog is likely to have made the association between your chant and eliminating.

Many owners make the mistake of continually taking a dog out before he really needs to go. Although they do so hoping that he won't soil the house, they are actually preventing him from developing the capacity to wait. Because housetraining is a matter of teaching the dog to control his bladder and bowels until he has access to the outdoors, taking the dog out too frequently slows the housetraining process.

The amount of time spent eliminating will be greatly reduced if your dog learns to associate the initial act of walking outdoors with the act of going potty. Have your dog earn playtime by pottying first and playing afterward. Avoid praising or rewarding with food, because the sensation of relief is a reward in itself. Besides, praise is exciting and may therefore distract him from his primary goal.

4. Make note of when you are taking your dog out and what he is doing. Document any accidents so you are alert to the problem times and can make needed adjustments. Take inventory of when your dog isn't going because, at least 90 percent of the time, he should go relieve himself when you take him out.

Also, write down the amounts and times you feed your dog, and any unusual consistency of his stool. If you later encounter a training or health problem, your notes may make the solution apparent.

5. Anytime the dog uses the house as a toilet, he has negated any previous good behavior. Every consecutive hour your dog spends wandering the house, sniffing and exploring without an accident, brings you closer to your goal of owning a dog who is repulsed by the notion of going in the house—in other words, a housetrained dog.

Clean up accidents thoroughly and neutralize the spot, making note of how you could have prevented the mishap.

If your dog has an accident:

a. Stop him in the act by startling him. Try tossing something at him or picking him up in midstream and carrying him outside.

b. Never correct the dog after the fact. Do scold yourself by saying "How could I have let that happen?"

c. Clean up messes immediately. Remove debris and blot up any moisture, then use a cleaning solution and finally treat the soiled area with an odor neutralizer.

If your dog lacks training . . .

a. Don't rely on or encourage him to tell you that he wants to go out. Dogs often indicate when they want to go outdoors and play, instead of when the need to eliminate. Moreover, many dogs will indicate frequently and always eliminate when taken to the potty area. This causes underdeveloped bladder and bowel control. So, if your dog is used to going out on demand to go potty, he may have to relieve himself immediately whether you're available or not. Don't encourage indication. Instead, train puppies to control their elimination with supervision, a proper diet and a reasonable "potty break" schedule. Once he's housetrained, you can insist that he bark, paw or ring a bell by bumping it with his nose before letting him out. But housetrained dogs don't need to be taught how or when to indicate. They'll do anything necessary to get your attention when an urgent need arises, or to hold it if you aren't available.

b. Don't let your dog out without supervision and assume that he relieved himself. Dogs enjoy playing, observing and investigating and often forget about eliminating when they're left alone outdoors. Even if your dog has just spent a lot of time outdoors, he may mess soon after he comes back inside.

c. Don't judge his capacity and trustworthiness by his behavior while crated. Dogs who can refrain from eliminating for long periods while they're in their cage or at night are not necessarily well on their way to being housetrained. The dog's metabolism slows down with inactivity, and so even a totally untrained dog may not soil for up to twelve hours when he's caged. Dogs aren't trained until they understand that it is okay to move about, explore and go potty outdoors, but must "hold it" as they move about and explore indoors.

Paper Training

If you own a small dog and you don't want to have to walk him outdoors, paper train. You'll need full-size newspapers (not tabloids) and a 16-square-foot, wire-mesh exercise pen, available from dog supply catalogs. Line the pen with newspapers opened flat out. After keeping the dog or pup in the fully-papered pen for a week anytime you aren't supervising or exercising, cover most of the area with neatly arranged newspaper and put a bed in the unpapered portion. Gradually reduce the papered portion to one full-size newspaper, overlapping at least five sheets to ensure proper absorption. Once he is pottying on the paper, open up the pen within a small room or hall with easy-to-clean floors. When he consistently soils on the paper, gradually give him access to the house, room by room, when you are able to supervise him. Shuttle him over to the papers if he attempts to go elsewhere. If he begins missing the paper to any degree, follow the confinement and umbilical cording procedure described for outdoor training, except take the dog to the paper, rather than the outdoors, to eliminate.

Once your dog eliminates on the paper, open up the pen within a small room with easy-to-clean floors.

Once trained, some paper trained dogs only go on their papers; others prefer the outdoors but will use papers if necessary. You can paper train a previously outdoor trained dog and vice versa, but you'll avoid extra work by deciding what process you want at the beginning.

The Well-behaved House Dog

If your dog isn't currently chewing, stealing, charging windows or jumping on counters and furniture, beware: Dogs who housetrain easily are in the greatest danger of acquiring nasty habits like these. And owners who don't worry that their dogs might soil tend to give undeserved freedom and, thus, the opportunity to misbehave.

If cigarettes, a lighter and ashtray were left at a child's bedside, you probably wouldn't be shocked if she eventually tried smoking. Similarly, prevent your dog from developing bad habits by cutting off early opportunities. Crate him when you're occupied, and umbilical cord or supervise him at all other times so you can intervene with a jerk of the leash or stomp on the floor if he gets a naughty thought.

Good Behavior Outside the Home

RIDING IN THE CAR

Good car travel manners ensure safety for both the driver and the dog. A dog's movement can obstruct your view and that, along with noise, can distract you. Dogs who stick their heads out the window expose their eyes to injury or, if you swerve or brake abruptly, may fall out of the car. Contain your dog during car rides so that he is unlikely to develop bad habits like barking and lunging. Also, in the event that you have an accident, your dog won't be thrown about the car or escape through a broken window and run into traffic. You'll also appreciate not having to clean smeared, dried, canine nostril fluid (nose prints) from your windows.

Contain and secure your dog during car rides by:

- crating

- using a store-bought Doggy Seat-belt

- installing a vehicle pet barrier

- tying a nonchewable leash to the seat belt fitting, allowing only enough slack for your dog to sit vulture-fashion

WALKING ON LEASH

Don't Heel your dog on lengthy, recreational walks. These "casual walks" don't call for the military precision of heeling. Relax and enjoy your walks, and use

sneakaways to keep your dog from walking ahead of you or pulling. You'll want to practice heeling, of course, because dogs who heel well are likely to be a pleasure to walk and easy to control even when they're not under order to heel.

VETERINARY, GROOMER AND KENNEL VISITS

Ensure that your dog has pleasant experiences and is under control by using all outings as excuses to test and improve his obedience skills. Control him in the car, invite him out, insist on nice walking manners, enforce commands in the building, hand him over to caretakers without fanfare and expect him to remain somewhat composed when he's returned to you. He will be more relaxed and others will delight in caring for their willing four-legged client.

Grooming

To be able to successfully (and peacefully) groom your dog, begin by acclimating him to handling of all areas of his head. Look in his eyes, ears and mouth, examine his feet (feel the toes, pads and nails) and body (run your hands along his legs, underbelly, chest and tail). Hold his collar with one hand so you can jerk it to settle a feisty pup. Consider grooming on a small elevated surface because your

Accustom your dog to sit for grooming or for an examination. While your dog is on a Sit-Stay, examine his eyes, ears, mouth and feet.

The Settle position: Grasp the dog's outer legs.

Continue holding his legs and slide the rear legs under your body.

Gently roll the legs under his body so he is lying on his side.

Grip his waist lightly between your knees and place your thumbs under his armpits.

dog will be less likely to fidget. Also, if the area allows, tie a leash to an overhead pipe or ceiling hook so that the snaps hang down just low enough to attach it to his collar to create a noose-like arrangement. And just like a professional groomer, *never* leave your dog unattended when noosed.

With a pup of at least 6 weeks or an adult dog that you'd like to groom while he's lying on his side, practice putting him in the Settle position. This procedure teaches relaxation, develops trust and ensures acceptance of grooming and handling. Kneel on the ground at the dog's side and reach around him as if you were giving a bear hug. Clasp his legs on the opposite side and gently roll him by moving his legs under his body and toward you. Then with your hand holding the rear leg, slide his bottom between your knees and straddle him. Place your hands, palms down, on his chest with your thumbs facing one another below his armpits to prevent him from wriggling away. Remain still and calm. When he relaxes, release him by saying Okay as you loosen your hold. Only do this procedure with pups under 4 months of age or with dogs who are non-aggressive. If you have reason to teach the Settle position to a feisty adolescent or adult dog, thorough sneakaway sessions and basic obedience are recommended first, to make them more pliable and surrendering.

chapter 6

Problem-Solving

Basics

If you haven't read and practiced the basic training techniques, and instead skipped to
this problem-solving section, I
sympathize. But the relationship between obedience and
problem-solving is like the relationship between diet and good
health. A proper diet doesn't
guarantee good health and obe-

dience doesn't guarantee a problem-free existence. Obedience is,
however:

1. the best insurance against the development of problems,

2. the simple solution for correcting problems,

3. preparation for the dog in learning to accept problem-solving
   techniques.

So, read the topics of interest, but I advise working the sneakaway and teaching the Come, Sit, Down and Stay before or while

following the recommended procedures. You may find that basic training alone will solve the problem.

Most problems require a step-by-step plan, usually including training procedures, corrective procedures and better management. The following recommendations will be referred to under the headings of several problems.

Swimming and retrieving are good exercises for your dog.

Medical Clearance Have your veterinarian confirm there is no medical reason for the problem.

More Exercise Provide your dog with vigorous aerobic exercise for a minimum of fifteen minutes, at least three times a week. You can jog your dog on foot or alongside a bike or have her continuously retrieve or swim. Consult your veterinarian and a breeder or other expert who is familiar with your breed and dog to answer specific exercise-related questions.

Proper Confinement Every dog needs a place where she can do no wrong in your absence. Kennels and crates are best suited for this purpose.

Umbilical Cording Tie your dog to your belt with a short leash in a way that gives you both freedom of movement. Your hands will be free so you can do what needs to be done and train your dog simultaneously.

Supervise Eliminate opportunities to misbehave by keeping your dog's every movement under surveillance.

Obedience Training Attain one-command control around all distractions, so that you'll be able to abort inappropriate behavior.

Mental Exercise Continually teach your dog new tasks—tricks, obedience or specialized work (hunting, herding and the like). You and your dog will develop a better relationship by pursuing challenging and stimulating goals together.

Calm Arrivals   Remain emotionally detached, even if your dog greets you with enthusiasm. Don't return the affection, until you've been in the house with her for at least fifteen minutes.

Set-up   Concoct a situation that would cause your dog to attempt a misbehavior when you are physically and mentally prepared to stop her.

Bitter Apple Correction   Hold the collar and/or the back of your dog's neck as you press the nozzle of the spray bottle against her lip line, then spritz. This correction must be initiated *while* the dog is misbehaving. She should never see the bottle in hand unless you are actually correcting.

Teach your dog new tasks to keep her mind alert.

Leash Jerk   Snap the leash quickly in the direction opposite of the misbehavior.

Startle Correction   Clap your hands together sharply, toss shaker cans, spray a water pistol between your dog's eyes or blast a boat horn to make her flinch away from a misbehavior she has just started or was contemplating.

Booby Traps   Set traps that will automatically correct your dog when triggered by her misbehavior—for example, strategically placed mousetraps, shaker cans or electronic Scat Mats.

Diaper   To keep your house clean while your dog learns to control her elimination, fashion a diaper for your dog by fastening a towel or bandanna with Velcro, tape or pins around her waist and tail. Or, use boy's underwear, sticking your dog's tail through the fly. Keep her leashed and supervised until you teach her to ignore it by using a jerk of the leash when she shows the least bit of interest.

Problem Analysis

If you've determined that the dog hasn't been given too much freedom too soon, you've done the proper

95

basic training and you still having problems, it's time to:

1. categorize the problem,
2. determine how you can quickly and safely stop your dog in the act of misbehavior,
3. commit yourself to consistently applying the solutions.

CATEGORIZE THE PROBLEM

Certain problems should never be disciplined. Annie and Ed's Cocker Spaniel has a problem with submissive urination; because the dog is so excited when they arrive home, it tinkles. They know that yelling, threatening and hitting only make it worse. Still, they have trouble hiding their exasperation. Their grumble, their posture and brusque movements reflect the tension that they feel. The dog's submission, and tinkling, increase. I recommended that they accept the inevitable leakage, turn their backs and enforce commands on-leash. By relaxing and focusing on enforcing routine obedience commands instead of their angry thoughts, the urination gradually subsided.

DISCIPLINE— RIGHT OR WRONG?

Many people think that the best way to solve problems is through discipline. But the truth is, most dogs are terrorized and confused by discipline, and the problems often grow worse as a result of the negative response. Discipline will only compound emotional problems such as submissive urination and separation anxiety. In fact, most dogs with problems were given too much freedom too quickly. If your dog cowers or looks shameful or guilty, she is most likely confused about your apparent mood swings rather than "telling" you something about her behavior. Regardless of the misbehavior, don't discipline your dog after the fact or walk around angrily; you'll have more success if you forget about discipline and start retraining your dog and rebuilding your communication skills.

COMMIT YOURSELF TO CONSISTENTLY APPLYING THE SOLUTIONS

Bitter Apple, leash jerks, cuffs, shaker cans or yelling can effectively deter misbehavior, but are cruel when used inappropriately. Consider this example: A student recently told me about his Husky Blade's digging problem. When he caught Blade digging, he tried a variety of corrections—spraying water, saying

"No," throwing shaker cans, taking the dog up to the hole and scolding him. But anytime Blade spent more than a few minutes in the yard, he would start again. The owner was sure the dog knew better by the way Blade cowered when he went out to correct him.

As soon as I heard that, I knew that it wasn't a matter of finding the right correction, but rather, improving the owner's timing. The facts are that Blade is given unsupervised freedom in diggable areas, sometimes digs endlessly without interruption or consequence and receives intermittent correction for digging. Blade doesn't understand that the intermittent corrections are related to his digging and is only learning to distrust his owner's erratic behavior.

Prevent problems by keeping personal belongings out of your dog's reach.

Remember that by definition, an inconsistent correction is too harsh.

General Problem-Solving Options

1. Don't let problems occur. Instead:

    a. keep your dog confined when you can't prevent misbehavior,

    b. put out of reach anything that is or may be tempting, such as paper, garbage, personal belongings and paraphernalia like remote controls,

    c. close off areas with problem-making potential; shut the kids' bedroom door so she can't confiscate their toys, or block off the living room so she can't see or hear the paper boy's approach.

2. Divert your dog's attention from bad behavior by distracting her or rechanneling her energy:

a. To curtail attempts to chew woodwork or to dig in the garden, encourage her to play with a toy,

b. offer food while acclimating a sensitive or ticklish dog to having her feet massaged,

c. give obedience commands in rapid-fire succession to stop barking, jumping up or nipping.

3. Build an aversion to misbehavior by correcting every attempt to misbehave:

a. Spritz a water pistol between your dog's eyes if she barks at you for attention during meals,

b. launch a shaker can at the rear of a dog who is looking for a spot to eliminate in the house,

c. spray Bitter Apple on the leash as your dog grabs at it,

d. set booby traps with snappy trainers, balloons or Scat Mats so that your dog's misbehavior triggers an immediate correction.

Common Problems
OVERCOMING FEAR

Our natural reaction is to console a fearful dog. Whether her phobia involves inanimate objects like garbage cans, loud or strange noises, other dogs, children, or places like the veterinarian's office, hallways or stairwells, reassurance only reinforces fear. Instead, ignore her panic and force her to concentrate on what she knows best. Teach reliable obedience, and give commands in rapid-fire sequence for two minutes or until she is relaxed, or at least responding automatically to Sit, Down, Stay and Come. Then initiate playtime by running, nudging, patting the ground or talking silly. Continue rapid-fire commands if she seems preoccupied by her fear. Practice first in situations in which she's uncomfortable but not panicked, then gradually progress to greater challenges.

Curtail attempts to chew or dig inappropriately by encouraging your dog to play with a toy.

If her phobia involves going up or down stairs or in or out of an enclosure, leash her and approach the source of her fear with confidence. For example, with stairs, grip the railing and progress up or down one step at a time, never looking at the dog. Repeat methodically and mechanically until your dog walks with you as she does around the block on leash. When possible, begin with just a few stairs or use a very wide stairway.

JUMPING UP

If your dog is thrilled when you or guests or family members arrive, you probably like her attitude but not the jumping that goes along with it. Such zealous greetings are actually taught by family members. When they shower your dog with affection upon entering the house, she isn't noting their love (she already knows that they love her), she is simply learning to act inappropriately.

First, human self-control is in order. Practice calm arrivals. Play, fun and enthusiasm are important parts of a well-balanced, bonded relationship, but should never be associated with people coming and going.

Don't encourage overzealous greet-ings—your own arrivals should be calm and uneventful.

Make it a habit to busy yourself doing other things, oblivious to your dog's prancing, barking, jumping or panting. Insist that guests and family members do the same. Within two weeks of practicing uneventful arrivals, you may find that the jumping up has entirely subsided.

If calm arrivals haven't cured your dog, continue practicing them but, in addition, try these tactics:

1. Teach the Wait command. Do you have complete control when you open a door and your dog sees

people on the other side? If she always listens to the Wait command, no matter how inviting the distraction on the other side of the door, you will no longer have to worry about, yell at, plead with or restrain your dog around guests.

2. Don't give your dog easy targets for jumping. Jumping on a moving target is very difficult, so ask people to shuffle into the dog as she begins jumping.

3. If she tends to jump on those who can't or won't shuffle, snap on a leash and step on it, so that she has only enough slack to begin jumping but will be jerked long before she is able to pounce on someone.

4. Teach and enforce the Off command (see Chapter 4, "Commands").

5. Establish control before attempting the Down-Stay. The Down-Stay is incompatible with jumping up and therefore a good prescription. Unfortunately, it's also the most difficult command to enforce with an excited dog. Begin by perfecting the Wait, then enforce the Off, next correct barking, and finally, after successfully completing those steps, focus on the Down-Stay.

SEPARATION ANXIETY

An overly-dependent dog gets frantically frustrated when she's separated from her owner. Continual barking, whining and howling, destruction of her or your living space and attempts to escape by chewing, digging and jumping over fences and out of windows are common responses to separation. In addition to causing expensive damage, many dogs injure themselves. When panicked, they are oblivious to the physical discomfort of laryngitis, bloody/raw gums and paws, broken teeth, self-mutilation caused by chewing and licking, and even broken limbs as a result of jumping out of windows.

After-the-fact corrections will confuse her and increase her anxiety. Consoling tones and gentle petting will only embed the neurosis. Instead:

1. provide regular, vigorous exercise,

2. teach reliable obedience to improve her ability to handle all sources of stress,

3. always ignore your dog as you leave and return, as lack of concern about separations is contagious,

4. practice three exercises to directly increase her tolerance of separations:

a. **Random tie-outs:** Tie her in new areas and insist that she remain quiet. Take your dog to indoor and outdoor areas, familiar and unfamiliar, filled with or absent of distractions. Silently tie her leash short to a stationary object and walk away for a few minutes. Try it while remaining in sight and also while out of sight. Correct noise making by tossing a shaker can, spraying her with water or spritzing her mouth with Bitter Apple. Concentrate on the areas in which your dog is most uncomfortable. Practice every other day for a half hour until she'll be silent regardless of where you leave her, where you go and how long you're gone.

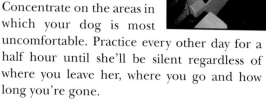

A dog who is too dependent on her owner will panic when separated.

b. **Out-of-sight Sit and Down-Stays** (see chapter 4): Practice fifteen- to twenty-minute Down-Stays with lots of distractions at least every other day.

c. **Whirling Dervish Departures:** Rush from room to room grabbing your keys, briefcase, jacket and so on. Zoom out the door and down the driveway, drive around the block, pull back in the garage and saunter into the house. Completely ignore your dog as you put your keys, jacket and paraphernalia away. Relax for a few minutes then repeat the frenzied departure and relaxed arrival over and over for an hour. Continue desensitizing your dog to comings and goings by repeating the pattern three times the first week, then once a week for a month.

Make it a habit to periodically confine your dog when you are home. Sequester her in a quiet area and place your recently worn sweatshirt or bathrobe on the floor on the other side of the closed door. If your smell emanates from the next room, she may not even realize it when you finally do leave. Give her her favorite toy only when you confine her. Make confinement more desirable by spitting on your hands and rubbing up the toy with your scent before every offering. Eliminate agitating noise created by neighbors or delivery people and tune out the TV and radio stations and their unsettling cacophony. Instead, create "white" noise by running a fan or playing radio static at low volume. Then, when you do actually leave, follow the same routine.

Despite these precautions, separation problems can periodically return, so memorize and apply these guidelines as needed.

Submissive Urination

Puppies and certain breeds are prone to emotional states in which they uncontrollably, and sometimes unconsciously, leak urine. If your dog has been given a clean bill of health by a veterinarian but wets when she greets people or is disciplined, she isn't having a housetraining problem. Although you cannot correct her problem, you can gradually diminish it by:

1. giving commands, thereby forcing your dog to focus on her responsibilities instead of her emotions,

2. keeping your dog leashed to enable nonemotional, silent correction of misbehaviors,

3. avoiding eye contact, talking and touching during emotional states,

4. making your entrances and greetings devoid of emotion,

4. making your entrances and greetings devoid of emotion,

5. not yelling, striking or getting angry at her.

Living with this behavior can be exasperating, and you may want to consider diapering your dog for the first thirty days so you don't have to continually clean up. Diaper your dog by pinning a bandanna or towel around her privates. Acclimate your dog to wearing the diaper and teach her not to remove it by umbilical cording and jerking the leash if she even sniffs at it. When she is totally uninterested in the diaper—usually after less than a week of umbilical cording—let her walk around the house unleashed as usual, without concern about dribbling.

With the worst submissive wetters, avoid vigorous petting, impassioned tones of voice and strong eye contact. Only interact with a superficial, brief pat, calm word or fleeting glimpses when her bladder is empty. When she consistently responds without tinkling, test her control after she's had water. Gradually try a warmer approach, but be ready to turn off the affection and issue a command if it's more than she can tolerate.

CAR PROBLEMS

When your dog is restrained in the car by crating, tying or seat belting, unruly behavior is unlikely to occur and easy to stop if it does. If your dog becomes disruptive, attach a leash to her collar to hold and jerk when necessary, as you drive.

If your dog gets carsick or refuses to go in, teach her to enter and exit the car on command. Leash her, open the car door or hatch and command her to go in as you give her a boost. Immediately invite her out with a Chin Touch–Okay, and repeat the procedure five times in a row, several times per day. Within a week she should be responding on command. Dogs who've been trained to readily jump in and out of the car on command are more relaxed about riding and less inclined toward motion sickness.

If your dog has a canine companion who likes riding, have them sit in the car together to develop a better association about being in the car. Or, try building the positive association with food: If your dog is a fairly neat chow hound, feed her in the parked car.

Dogs who are trained to readily get in and out of the car on command are more relaxed travelers.

If your dog has a tendency to get carsick, however, don't feed her for three hours before a ride. Also experiment with placing her in different spots in the car; there may be a location that won't induce sickness because it changes the view, or improves the airflow or smoothness of the ride. If nothing works, ask your veterinarian about using motion sickness medication.

BEGGING

It may take only one tidbit for your clever dog to be convinced that your meals are better than hers and that you're willing to share if she begs. You may not care if she begs from you, especially if you have the control to command her to down-stay to prevent her from begging from others. But, if you find begging totally intolerable, follow these suggestions:

1. Feed her only dog food and only in her dish, rather than sharing goodies or feeding from your hands or a plate.

2. Don't look at her when you eat.

3. If you want your dog to down-stay during meals:

    a. teach the Down-Stay as described in chapter 4,

    b. tie her up away from the table during mealtimes for two months,

    c. enforce the Down-Stay while tied for one month.

If you've started this bad habit, the dog's can be broken, but can yours?

When a dog is alone all day in the house, she gets bored. She is trapped and has no hands with which to do arts and crafts; but she does have plenty of senses yearning to be indulged. When given too much freedom too soon, she will quickly discover the joys of hunting for household treasures too often left easily accessible by negligent humans.

A dog who steals when you're home is entertained by seeking you out to show off the stuff that she's found. Like taxes and death, the predictable outcome is that she becomes the immediate center of your attention as you bound out of the recliner and chase her around.

Police the canine clepto by:

1. incarceration—crating,
2. chain gang—umbilical cording,
3. surveillance—keeping your eyes glued to her.

Don't be a victim:

1. Keep the garbage out of reach.
2. Close cabinets and closets and put laundry away.
3. Teach the Drop It or Leave It command.

Dispense justice fairly:

1. Never correct stealing after the fact.
2. Upon discovering the misbehavior, leash your dog, invite her to make the same mistake and correct it with a leash jerk.

CRATE SOILING

Although dogs usually won't mess in their crates, some do. Occasional accidents shouldn't concern you, but if it happens with some frequency try these suggestions:

1. Remove all bedding from the crate so there is nothing other than her body to absorb the mess.
2. Use a smaller crate so she only has enough room to turn in place.

3. Teach her to go in and out of the crate on command (see "Confinement," in chapter 5).

4. Put her food and water in the open crate to encourage a better association about being in there; remove it when she's enclosed.

*A small crate
without bedding
can help to deter
crate soiling.*

CURTAIL RITUALS THAT PRECEDE SOILING

Unless your dog has a physical problem, crate-soiling is invariably preceded by a ritual like whining, barking, pawing, digging, chewing on bars, or circling, turning, sitting, standing or lying down repeatedly.

To solve the problem, begin by confining your dog when you are home so you can correct the ritual as soon as it starts. Stop noise making (barking, howling or whining) and destructive behavior (chewing, digging or pawing) by using a leash jerk or shaker can as suggested in "Introducing Your Dog to the Crate," page 80. Concentrate on eliminating the most pronounced behavior first, and you'll find that minor noise making and less destructive behaviors will decrease, too. As a result, the dog will relax, rest and not soil.

If these suggestions fail to work, I recommend you buy a grate so the urine and excrement can drop to the floor of the crate. It is easier to clean up, the dog won't get messy and the odor is less offensive.

House-soiling

Even if you keep your dog in good health, alter her, and commit to a lengthy and an ever-watchful program of housetraining and basic training, there is no guarantee that house-soiling will never be a problem. No matter how well entrenched a house-soiling problem may be, it can be solved by:

1. treating the dog as totally untrustworthy, just as you would an 8-week-old pup,

2. doing daily vigorous obedience training so that the dog is accustomed to taking direction from you.

If you are experiencing problems with a dog who is under 8 months of age, or who has been in your house less then six months, you should not have given her the freedom to misbehave. Lack of supervision and confinement gives a dog the green light to use the house as a toilet. Close that window of opportunity.

Lack of supervision and confinement gives a dog a green light to misbehave.

An occasional dog will not be averse to going potty while she's umbilical corded. The advantage when working with this type is, once she's trained not to go while umbilical corded, she will quickly become reliably housetrained. Correct her with a jerk immediately if she attempts to let loose in the house.

Assume that if she messed up once, she will do so again. This way she can't disappoint you. If your dog is a recidivist, you'll be ready for action; if she isn't, you'll be pleasantly surprised. Train her vigorously on new obedience routines and commands fifteen minutes every other day. Give her vigorous exercise the other days.

Do *not* permit your dog unsupervised freedom in the house for as long as she has been violating good housetraining habits. When she is out of confinement, keep your eyes riveted to her and be ready to launch a shaker can or something equally startling at her if she begins any actions that precede soiling, like sniffing or circling. Don't yell or in any way draw attention to your part in this corrective procedure.

To make your spying pay off faster, set her up so you can deliver more corrections. Rub down another dog with a towel and drape the scented towel on a chair, bed or door knob. The suspicion that another dog has been in her house may cause her to mark. This time, though, you'll be ready to stop her. Also, be on the defensive if you give her the opportunity to eliminate outdoors but she does not because she's distracted. Rather than crate her, follow her around the house, waiting for her to consider going indoors. Distract or correct her if she starts sniffing or circling with intent. Say nothing and spray her with water, jerk the leash if it is attached or toss a shaker can at her rear end.

If your dog only eliminates in a certain area when you aren't watching (such as behind the couch or upstairs), block off the area or booby trap it with balloons, mousetraps or Scat Mats.

When, after weeks or months of following, your dog has developed an aversion to going indoors, gradually allow her unsupervised freedom.

If you loathe having her confined, but cannot supervise her 100 percent of the time, consider diapering as described under "Submissive Urination," above, so she cannot soil the house.

PROJECTILES

Although I explain to my students the use of the shaker can for problem-solving and the throw-chain to improve their dog's response to obedience commands, I personally feel projectile corrections are overused. Frequently, owners rely on projectiles when they have failed to spend the time and energy to master basic dog training fundamentals. Of course, projectiles are great shortcuts if they produce satisfactory results with a fraction of the effort, but that rarely happens.

I advise using projectiles only after practicing sneakaways, teaching commands and reducing problems using the traditional, on-leash methods described in chapters 3 and 4.

If you've used projectiles with limited success, stop using them at least until you 1) improve obedience, 2) plug up the goofing gaps so your dog can't make mischief in your absence and 3) set her up on-leash so that each time she makes the wrong decision, you can stop her. Finally, exercise caution as you start giving your dog more freedom. And to ensure that your dog will be responsive to your mild corrections, enforce the no-pulling rule.

Finally, be aware that edible products like rawhide, pig ears and cow hoofs increase your dog's thirst and can upset her stomach and even get lodged in the intestines—a medical emergency. If your dog is having house-soiling problems or gets tense in the presence of these edible items, get rid of them. Of course, if you want to give them and they keep your dog busy with no side effects, consult your breeder or veterinarian.

EATING STOOL (COPROPHAGIA)

So, your dog has a thing for poop? Her own, or that of other animals? Don't be embarrassed. This tendency is so common that virtually every dog training book devotes a section to it. Nutritional deficiency can be the cause for this behavior, so you should first consult a veterinarian. As a rule however, coprophagia is simply a behavioral problem.

Preventative Measures

If you accompany your dog outdoors on-leash and command her to go eliminate, you'll be able to clean-up after her immediately and stop a bad habit before it starts. Even habitual stool eaters may lose their taste and fascination for it if they're not given an opportunity to eat stool for many months.

Teach Repulsion

Teach repulsion by setting your dog up on-leash. The procedure is similar to the one used to teach Drop It and Leave It, but in this situation, don't use a command. Take her to the waste of preference and use a silent Bitter Apple spray if she tries to munch. Repeat this setup daily by approaching the foul temptation with her on-leash, ready to spritz Bitter Apple in her mouth as she attempts to snatch a nugget. Don't allow her off-leash until she refrains for at least one to two weeks. The same procedure can be used if the dog likes to roll in smelly stuff—except spray her mouth when she is sniffing the "perfume" before she actually rolls.

From the Medicine Cabinet

If your dog only eats her own stool you can add Forbid (available at veterinarians) to her food. Unfortunately, it's not a long-term solution; she'll resume the habit when you take her off the medicine.

MOUTHING

Mouthing problems take many forms. We expect pups to mouth and bite during teething from 3 to 6 months of age. But, be warned: Some pre- and post-teething pups mouth as obsessively as their 3- to -6-month-old counterparts. Natural though it may be, you must stop mouthing of flesh and valuables regardless of when it occurs, so that it does not become habitual.

Here are some tips:

1. Give your puppy wash rags that have been wetted, twisted out of excess water and frozen. Chewing on these relieves the discomfort of teething. Replace with a fresh one when it begins to thaw.

2. Give your puppy plenty of exercise, keep her leashed indoors and outdoors and elicit play with proper toys.

Correct mouthing by:

1. screeching "ouch," jerking the leash and eliciting play with the proper toy,

2. spritzing Bitter Apple on the dog's lip line while gripping her collar with your free hand.

Correct chasing or nipping of children by:

1. never allowing unsupervised contact between puppies and children,

2. intervening to curtail disrespectful, inappropriate actions from puppy or child.

Keep a fairly long leash attached to the pup so you can jerk it as the child says "ouch." This teaches your puppy to stop biting when the child screams out; over time, she may stop nipping entirely.

BITING

Dogs bite to get our attention, relieve frustration or change our behavior. Whether it's playful, fear-driven or dominant, get better control of the dog with obedience. Don't ever allow her to be unleashed in a situation where she could threaten anyone. Be aware of the signs of impending aggression, such as making hard eye contact, stiffening, shifting weight forward, sticking tail out, growling, fast whining, or signs of interest, excitement or arousal.

When in doubt as to what your dog's behavior indicates, make her focus on commands. The time to get control is well before she reaches a highly agitated state; when her adrenaline is peaking, she'll be oblivious to your attempts to correct her. This requires acute and constant supervision by a proficient handler.

Unfortunately, some owners appreciate (consciously or unconsciously) a dog's aggression and reinforce it by rewarding it or denying it's existence. Most dog bite injuries and aggressive-dog euthanasia could have been avoided with proper supervision, socialization, training and intervention by an owner who recognized the warning signs and instantly stopped inappropriate behavior.

CHEWING

When left to her own devices, a dog is certain to chew up your possessions. If you prefer not to learn first-hand about the dangers of giving too much freedom too soon, puppy-proof your house by keeping it tidy, keeping doors closed and

Give your dog an appropriate toy to play with to help diminish unwanted chewing.

personal items out of reach and, as a preventative measure, smearing Bitter Apple cream on tempting woodwork and electrical cords. Confine your puppy in a safe place when you can't supervise her. Finally, keep her leashed and correct her while she's in the act of chewing by:

111

1. jerking the leash away from what she's chewing on,

2. giving a spray of Bitter Apple in the mouth as you hold the collar,

3. startling the pup with a sharp hand clap or shaker can, then encouraging her to play with an appropriate toy.

Note that certain items can increase problems with inappropriate chewing behavior. Avoid giving your dog personal items to chew on, like slippers, socks, gloves or towels. If your dog is attracted to the family's stuffed toys, don't give her soft, stuffed dog toys. If she is attracted to rugs or tassels, don't provide her with rope- or raglike toys.

If an older dog suddenly begins chewing on your possessions, give her plenty of exercise and appropriate items to chew, continue vigorous obedience and return to crating and supervising.

DIGGING

Digging is a survival mechanism for dogs; plus, it's a lot of fun. Dog's don't dig because they are dominant, belligerent, unaware of authority or out of control. They do it to make a cool or warm place to lie down. Females dig to make a nestlike den for their puppies. Interesting smells in the soil and the wonderful feeling of vigorous burrowing and dirt in their toes is hard for any dog to resist. Digging and coprophgia are practically the only problems that cannot be prevented, lessened or solved with obedience training (although sometimes training, because it relieves boredom, indirectly reduces the behavior). That's why monitoring your dog and correcting digging attempts is an ongoing process—you aren't fighting your dog, you are fighting nature.

To stop or prevent digging:

1. Leave your dog in a run or tied out on concrete, patio block or a similar, undiggable surface when you can't supervise.

2. Make sure her environment is comfortable. Provide fresh water and shelter from heat, cold, wind and rain.

3. Give her plenty of exercise so that she doesn't seek aerobic activity from digging.

4. Fill previously dug holes with dog feces. Most dogs won't return to dig in that hole, although some dogs will simply dig new holes.

To correct digging, you must use extreme vigilance in monitoring your dog. Watch your dog, and when she begins digging, startle her without saying a word by:

1. Jerking the leash (if it is attached). If you tie your dog, attach a second leash that is long enough for you to hold and jerk.

2. Blasting a boat horn. Out of respect for your neighbors, only use this if you live in a very rural area.

3. Tossing a shaker can at the dog.

BARKING

Although no one would object to your dog barking at Jack the Ripper, many people find a barking dog to be a nuisance. Out of respect for other household mem-

Correct barking, rather than appease a noisy dog.

bers, neighbors and tenants, I've always stopped almost all barking I hear. The result is a dog who still barks, but only for good reason. Barking is a highly natural tendency for some dogs. If they are ignored, they are encouraged to be increasingly vocal. Many owners unintentionally reinforce excessive barking by attempting to silence a dog by petting her or giving her a toy.

Dogs often use barking as a device to drive away or attract people, animals and objects. Correct the barking rather than trying to appease the dog by giving her the food she is barking for or telling the neighbor to keep his dog away from the common fence. If you reward the barking, it is going to occur with more frequency and intensity.

To correct barking, even if it is only a problem in your absence, teach the dog to be quiet on command when she's standing next to you (see "Other Important Commands," in chapter 4). If your dog will obey the Quiet command no matter what the distractions, barking in your absence will usually subside. If she doesn't, find out exactly when and why she is barking. Record her with a tape recorder when you leave, ask a neighbor about her habits and spy on her. If she is not barking at outside noises, separation anxiety (discussed above) is probably the problem.

If your dog is barking at outside noises:

1. Use opportunities when you are home to teach her not to bark at outside noises. Keep her leash attached and periodically knock on the walls and create a myriad of other strange sounds. Say nothing as you run over to correct with Bitter Apple or to cuff her under the jaw. Don't worry that the dog will stop barking at important things; I've never known a former excessive-barker who was able to resist vocalizing about anything suspicious.

2. In your absence, keep the dog in a covered crate in a noise-insulated room with a fan or other generated white noise. Occasionally crate her when you are home to make sure she is fuss-free or to correct her if she is fussy.

3. In extreme cases, you may want to investigate these options:

   a. Anti-bark collars emit a warning buzz when the collar is activated by vibrations caused by the dog's vocalization. The collar will deliver timely correction if the dog continues to make noise after the warning. The two most popular collars correct by delivering a mist of annoying citronella at the dog's muzzle or a mild electric shock.

b. Anti-anxiety medication (see your veterinarian to find out if your dog is a good candidate and to discuss benefits and risks).

c. A surgical procedure known as "debarking" will muffle the barking sound. Note that the vocal cords can heal back together, and if they do, the dog's bark will return to normal.

Shortcuts

Some shortcuts make your job easier with virtually no risk. For example, invisible fencing will help make a trained dog much more reliable about staying in the yard. Altering, in addition to its health benefits, can aid in solving problem behaviors. Remember that immediately after surgery is a great time to train your dog—she is likely to be at her most willing and attentive.

Instead of driving us closer to our goal, however, shortcuts may simply mask the real problem. Therefore, postpone using electricity, surgery or drugs until other options have been exhausted.

Shock collars, cutting vocal cords, extracting teeth from biting dogs or behavioral pharmacology may be your only recourse *after:*

1. rectifying such contributing imbalances as lack of exercise, improper diet, teasing and the like,

2. teaching and perfecting basic obedience for one to three months,

3. seeking out and following the advice of a dog training professional who can show you how to solve perplexing problems.

Follow Negatives with Positives

Want to deepen your bond with your dog, improve her obedience, increase her tendency to look to you for direction and lessen the chance she'll repeat misbehaviors? Simply follow negatives with positives: If she is doing something naughty, don't just tell her to stop it. Follow corrections for misbehavior with three to six

115

commands. For example, use Sit, Down or Come. Instead of feeling deprived for not being allowed to make mischief, she will feel a greater connection to you.

To apply the "follow negatives with positives" theory, try this special exercise using the Leave It command. Take a soup bone and lay it on the ground. Leash your dog and walk her up to it. As she displays interest, command Leave It as you give a quick, sharp jerk. Don't pull or drag her away. Command Sit, praise her, release her and then command Down. Praise, release, call Come and back up. Arrange the leash, command Heel, take three running steps and halt. The entire process should take less than thirty seconds. As you repeat the exercise, time yourself to confirm your concentration, efficiency and intensity.

As you practice this exercise, most dogs will lose their fascination for the less-than-desirable behavior, whether it's jumping up, barking, digging or chewing. The best you can hope for with some dogs, however, is that they will obey when asked—which, when you think about it, is probably a huge and welcome improvement.

Finding Time to Train

I had a dilemma. I wanted to train my dog BJ everyday. My 8-year-old Tibetan Spaniel had just finished her breed Championship title, and I was eager to get her obedience trial career started. But I toyed with that intention many times during the 5½ years that I owned her, only to see day-to-day life take over and my dog training motivation dissipate. When I'd trained my first two dogs about twenty years earlier, I had practiced right after school Monday through Friday and first thing in the morning on weekends. With my next dog, because I was eager to finish her obedience titles quickly, I put her through three sessions each day.

Over the years, I had become a part of a small, informal network of dog training buddies who practiced frequently. Unfortunately, I moved away and lost that support. And although I planned on training BJ before or after teaching my classes, I always found other things to do.

Maybe you too have felt my same frustration of having set a goal but failing to take the steps to achieve it—and maybe my solution will help you. I finally pledged to work with my dog twice a day, putting in at least ten minutes per session. Doing one session first thing in the morning proved to be my key to success. I found I actually looked forward to a more thorough evening session only when I trained in the morning. By committing to the morning session, I get double the benefit, with a fraction of the effort. While I dress, straighten up and prepare for the day's work, I have her do Stand-Stays (her weakest exercise) and keep my eyes glued to her. I enforce several Stay commands, each three to five minutes in duration. When I return to release her from one Stand-Stay, we do a little heeling, a trick or two and an assortment of other obedience commands. In about sixty seconds she is back on a Stay, while I do my morning chores. Then we repeat the routine. BJ gets about twenty minutes of training, and we both have a blast.

True, it takes me about five minutes longer to get ready in the morning, but I consider it time well spent. I leave for the day with a sense of accomplishment and anticipation for later practice. This contrasts nicely with the feelings of remorse (about not training), dread

BOOBY TRAPS

Booby traps are setups the dog triggers through misbehavior. Booby traps are most successful with dogs who are generally well behaved and somewhat timid. The great benefit to using booby traps is that bad behavior gets corrected even when you aren't watching every second.

Mousetraps or Snappy Trainers (mousetraplike paddles) are one solution. They can be strategically placed on furniture, garbage cans and other areas where your dog isn't allowed. Make the traps less obvious by covering them with a sheet of newspaper or other lightweight drape. Just make sure that the dog's misbehavior will trip the trap and that you'll be able to reset the trap quickly and quietly, so that repeated attempts will yield consistent results.

After the training phase, if your dog is indeed very startled by booby traps, you can leave them set while you're gone and therefore not able to reset them.

Scat Mats are another good solution. These pads can be placed around taboo objects like plants as well as on counters or furniture to deliver an unpleasant but harmless sensation when they are stepped on or touched. They're relatively expensive but are very effective and are widely available at pet shops or by mail order.

(because I expect performance she hasn't been trained to give), guilt (as the day is slipping away) and being overwhelmed (because I know that I'm not taking steps to reinforce the learning process).

Just think of the opportunities—while you are walking, feeding, grooming taking your dog to the veterinarian or as you're talking on the phone—to throw in some obedience work to keep it fresh in your mind and your dog's.

chapter 7

Owning and Training Multiple Dogs

So you feel guilty leaving your pet home alone all day when you're at work and think a canine companion is the perfect answer?

If you think that owning two dogs would cut your workload, think again. Two dogs are more than double the work and trouble.

Dogs who get along with one another can become fast friends. However, they may choose to bond with each other at the exclusion of you. If you have two dogs, teach them to accept being crated separately and to obey the Down-Stay while the other dog is being petted, played with, groomed, fed and taken in the car.

Two dogs together are inclined to make mischief that they wouldn't think of on their own.

When two dogs are together they are inclined to make mischief that they wouldn't think of on their own. One dog instigates a misbehavior, the other observes it and the possibilities for catastrophes are endless. Unfortunately, dogs rarely entertain themselves by practicing the behaviors you *want* them to learn. Instead of learning just to chew on their toys, they just learn to chew. Instead of learning where to relieve themselves, they learn to go relieve themselves everywhere. As the human, expect to train the dog yourself, because he'll never get the rules straight if you have him rely on the directions of another canine.

On the other hand, maybe you have the time for and interest in getting another dog, but are hesitant because Betsy seems to enjoy being the only child. Even well-established dogs usually adjust quite readily to a new addition.

Introducing a New Dog to Your Home

For the introductory period—the first week or two—keep the new dog confined when you're away and leashed when you're home and in the presence of your first dog. That way, if the new dog gets too rambunctious or nosy, you can silently stop him with a sharp jerk of the leash.

Dogs make a lot of noise as they wrestle, play and establish rules with one another. They do not usually seriously harm one another. Whenever possible, use the leash to control your dogs. Yelling at the most dominant dog tends to make him even pushier because he thinks that you, too, are displeased with the submissive one.

If you are concerned with aggressive displays from either dog, keep both leashed and contact a professional who can help advise on the introduction and training.

Handy Tips for Working with Two Dogs

1. Have a general "call name" to address both dogs—"kids," "girls," "monsters," etc.

2. When asking one dog to wait or stay on the sideline and the other to work on the Heel, Come, Front, Down or Sit command, reduce confusion by using a smooth Chin Touch with a step forward and tension on the leash to move the working dog forward. When your face is out of direct view of the sidelined dog, quietly give commands to the working dog.

Practice heeling both dogs.

3. Consider using hand signals to initiate commands, thereby further reducing confusion to the sidelined dog.

4. Keep both dogs leashed so that you can control their actions silently; repeated commands multiply confusion.

   Practice these specific exercises:

   a. At the door (house, car, yard gate, kennel)

      both dogs wait,

      both dogs go through together on command,

      one dog waits while the other is invited through.

   b. Heeling

      heel both dogs on left side,

      heel one dog while the other dog stays on the sidelines.

   c. Recall one dog

      call one dog's name,

121

*Stand, Sit and
Down-Stay are
beautifully demon-
strated by three
well-trained dogs.*

when he looks at you, use a beckoning hand
signal and reel him in,

use the opposite hand when calling the other
dog.

**CHOOSING A DOG
TRAINER OR SCHOOL**

Whether you are looking for
professional, in-person guidance,
or socialization for you and your
canine, there are many dog training programs and private instructors available. Gather names from
the phone book and newspaper and
by asking your veterinarian, humane
society, groomer, kennel, friends,
neighbors, coworkers or relatives
for recommendations.

Call the school and ask questions
about class curriculum, training
philosophy, location, number of
years in business, class size, instruc-
tor qualifications and cost. If you
are satisfied with your phone conversation, observe a class.

Note: When you call one dog,
both dogs will probably respond. Never pet the dog who
wasn't called—turn your back
to him or elbow him away as
you pet the other briefly. Walk
away and try it again.

d. Stays

both dogs stay,

one dog works, one dog stays.

Note: You should keep one eye
on the dog commanded to stay
as you work with the other dog.
Should the dog asked to stay
break, quietly say Okay to the
working dog as you rush over to
correct the staying dog.

part four

Beyond the Basics

chapter 8

Resources

Books

Ammen, Amy. *Training in No Time*. New York: Howell Book House, 1995.

Baer, Ted. *Communicating with Your Dog*. Hauppauge, N.Y.: Barron's Educational Series, Inc., 1989.

Benjamin, Carol Lea. *Dog Problems*. New York: Howell Book House, 1989.

————. *Dog Training for Kids*. New York: Howell Book House, 1988.

————. *Mother Knows Best*. New York: Howell Book House, 1985.

————. *Surviving Your Dog's Adolescence*. New York: Howell Book House, 1993.

Bohnenkamp, Gwen. *Manners for the Modern Dog*. San Francisco: Perfect Paws, 1990.

Dibra, Bashkim. *Dog Training by Bash*. New York: Dell, 1992.

Dunbar, Ian, PhD, MRCVS. *Dr. Dunbar's Good Little Dog Book*. James & Kenneth Publishers, 2140 Shattuck Ave., #2406, Berkeley, CA 94704. (510) 658-8588. Order from the publisher.

Dunbar, Ian, PhD, MRCVS, and Gwen Bohnenkamp. Booklets on Preventing Aggression, Housetraining, Chewing, Digging, Barking, Socialization, Fearfulness and Fighting. James & Kenneth Publishers. Order from the publisher; address above.

Evans, Job Michael. *People, Pooches and Problems.* New York: Howell Book House, 1991.

Fraser, Jacqueline and Amy Ammen. *Dual Ring Dog.* New York: Howell Book House, 1991.

Kilcommons, Brian and Sarah Wilson. *Good Owners, Great Dogs.* New York: Warner Books, 1992.

McLennan, Bardi. *Puppy Care and Training: An Owner's Guide to a Happy Healthy Pet.* New York: Howell Book House, 1996.

McMains, Joel M. *Dog Logic—Companion Obedience.* New York: Howell Book House, 1992.

Rutherford, Clarice and David H. Neil, MRCVS. *How to Raise a Puppy You Can Live With.* Loveland, Colo.: Alpine Publications, 1982.

Volhard, Jack and Melissa Bartlett. *What All Good Dogs Should Know: The Sensible Way to Train.* New York: Howell Book House, 1991.

Videos

Ammen, Amy. *Aggression in Dogs.* Amiable Dog Training, P.O. Box 93907, Milwaukee, WI 53203. (888) 875-4321. Order from the publisher.

———. *Basic Training.* Amiable Dog Training. Order from the publisher; address above.

———. *Come Here and Stay Home.* Amiable Dog Training. Order from the publisher; address above.

———. *Dual Ring Dog.* Amiable Dog Training. Order from the publisher; address above.

———. *Novice Dog Training.* Amiable Dog Training. Order from the publisher; address above.

———. *Open Dog Training.* Amiable Dog Training. Order from the publisher; address above.

————. *Puppy Training.* Amiable Dog Training. Order from the publisher; address above.

————. *Utility Dog Training.* Amiable Dog Training. Order from the publisher; address above.

Trainers

Association of Pet Dog Trainers
P.O. Box 3734
Salinas, CA 93912
(408) 663-9257

American Dog Trainer's Network
161 West 4th St.
New York, NY 10014
(212) 727-7257

National Association of Dog Obedience Instructors
2286 E. Steel Rd.
St. Johns, MI 48879